Remembering Catharine

Frances Maber

A catalogue record for this book is available from the National Library of Australia

Copyright © 2019 Frances Maber – Author
Copyright © 2019 Paul Moncrieff - Illustrations

All rights reserved.

ISBN: 1 876922 36 2
ISBN-13: 978-1-876922-36-8

Linellen Press
265 Boomerang Road
Oldbury, Western Australia
www.linellenpress.com.au

For William

Contents

Contents v
Author's Note vii
Introduction 1
The Soft Green Patch 3
Angry Sky 9
Cinnamon and Gold 17
Fading Gold 31
Four Stripes 42
Destructive Darkness 47
City Dirt – Foggy Skies 52
Wonderful Colourful Sea 65
Colours of a New Land 72
Drawn Thread Stitches 81
Rosy Days 91
Picture a Growing Town 105
Gold Dust Isn't Golden 115
Legal Matters 123
Life is Multi Coloured 128
Salt of the Earth 149
The Silken Cord 161
Coda 164
Bibliography 165
Acknowledgments 166
About the Author 168

Author's Note

Remembering Catharine is an exercise in imaginative biography – a term used by Professor Manning Clark during his final Boyer Lecture in 1976.

It is fiction based on the few facts known about Catharine and her family.

Underpinning the writing is a basic rule: if a character is fictitious then there is no surname.

That rule was broken once only – Mrs O'Reilly. It will be obvious to the reader why she had to be addressed that way.

All other characters with surnames were real people. The fiction exists in the interaction between Catharine and those people.

Introduction

I like to sit in the sun - it warms my hands. I hate my hands. They're twisted and lumpy.

I love to sew. I learnt about needlework when I was very young. If my hands weren't twisted and ugly I'd sit in the sun and retell my life by making a beautiful quilt for my bed. It would amaze with gentle colours, brilliant colours and every shade of black murk. The patches would be of different shapes, some just fabric, others over-embroidered.

To finish the quilt off, I'd make a wonderful cord of coloured silks and use it to link the patches, showing how to follow my story The patches have to be read in the right order just like the pages in a book.

I'll never make that quilt but I can plan it.

My first patch will be a soft green circle and on it I'll embroider my name *Catharine Jane Salter* surrounded by tiny white and golden flowers. It will be the centre of the quilt.

The Soft Green Patch

I was born in a tiny village in Kilkenny. I don't remember Mam, she died before I was walking. We lived in a house with one room. There was a bed I shared with Lizzie and a fireplace for cooking. Lizzie was my big sister, she called me Kitty. Sometimes she took me for a walk to a quiet place where there weren't many trees but there were square stones sticking out of the ground. We didn't bother with them. We walked past them to a patch of soft grass where we sat and picked tiny daisies. When we had enough my sister made daisy-chains, one for my head and one for her own. It was a fiddly job. I couldn't do it so I played games. Once I tried jumping over the big stones till I fell and hurt my knee. Lizzie kissed it better and showed me names on the stones. She explained about graves. She was always sad when we visited that place.

We didn't see a lot of Da. He had a donkey cart. He was a carter.

He'd pick up parcels from a farm and deliver them to another farm or to a village where he'd get another job. It often meant that he was away from home for a long time. When he came home he slept on the floor by the fire.

One of Da's best jobs came from a farm on the edge of the village. He worked free for that man so that Lizzie could attend the Hedge School at the farm. The teacher was the farmer's eldest son. This young man had crooked legs and couldn't work in the fields.

When Lizzie went to school she took me with her. The School Master let me stay and play with other children on the farm.

By the time I was old enough for school Lizzie had died. She got very sick. Lots of people in the village were sick too. I looked after her and tried to keep her warm by snuggling up against her in bed. It did no good. When she died I gave Da her clean shift but her dress and woollen jacket disappeared. An old lady wrapped my Lizzie in her shift and they carried her away to that lovely quiet green place and buried her. I hated that place and never went there again, even when I found out that my Mam was buried there too. There was no stone with Lizzie or Mam's name on it.

My Da didn't know what to do about me. He couldn't leave me at home because I was too small even to get water from the pump. Once he took me with him on the donkey cart but I couldn't keep up so he asked the farmer's wife for help. She took me in and said she'd find a job for me when I was a bit bigger. Sometimes I got to sit in for lessons at the school. I loved learning to read but I was bad at writing. I hated the noise when I scratched on the slate. After school I collected wood for the fire and went into the lanes to find greens for the stew. In the evenings I learnt to sew – easy things at first but I wanted to learn how to do beautiful stitches like the farmer's wife.

"Sure," she said, "you'll do it if you practise, Kitty."

Da's donkey died so he had to give up carting. He found a job at a Big House a long way from the village. They offered him work on the farm and said we could live in a small shed near the stables. I said goodbye to the village and to the School Master's family. They gave me two gifts. One was an old book about a man called Abraham. I loved that book: it was MINE, the first thing I had ever owned. The second gift was a box of needles and threads but we had no lamp in the shed so I couldn't sew.

I made up my mind to remember what I'd learnt. I'd try to read anything I saw. Sacks that I slept on had words on them and sometimes paper blew out of the Big House. If anything had words I spelt them out. Da thought I was very clever.

Living near that Big House taught me many tricks. I soon knew that it was better if no one ever saw me. The servants inside and around the House were a mixed bunch and none of them were children, though the gardener's boy wasn't much older'n me nor was one girl in the kitchen. Age had nothing to do with it. They were servants, I was a nuisance who was fed without earning it. They didn't like it. They'd swear at me or knock me out of the way. I was much smaller than all of them. They said I was too small to ever be any use. When they heard Da call me Kitty they started making cat noises or hissing at me. One even turned her fingers into claws and said she'd scratch me if I came near her.

It was different in the fields. The people who worked there knew my Da and were kind to me. I learnt quickly to follow down the rows when vegetables were being pulled and pick up any small pieces left behind. I was good at picking low growing fruit and they didn't mind if I ate some. When the barley was cut, they taught me to glean and to rake the dry stalks together before the stooks were made. It was fun.

At the end of harvest there was a party in the barn. Da took me and lifted me high on a pile of sacks where I would be out of the way but could see everything. Everyone was dressed in their best clothes and when the fiddler started they all joined the dance.

For the first time I saw some of the people who lived in the house. Da said the owners weren't there, though there was a very grand lady with keys hanging from the waist of her deep blue dress. There was a man even more grand who never smiled but watched everything. The grand lady noticed me and came over and asked my name. "Catharine Jane Salter," I said.

"When you speak to me, child, you must call me ma'am."

That scared me.

"How old are you?"

"Nearly ten ma'am. Da knows."

She smiled and turned away. Later I saw her talking to the very grand man and he talked to the overseer of the farm and he talked to my Da. I felt sure I'd done something wrong.

After the party when Da and I went back to our shed, he told me what it was all about. Paddy, the farm overseer, had noticed me in the fields and knew that I was very strong for my size. He had mentioned me to the very grand man. He was the Butler and he told the lady with the keys. She was the Housekeeper and she chose servants to work in the Big House. They needed an extra scullery maid so they were going to give me a trial. It was all because The Family was arriving soon and there would be lots of food to prepare and dishes to wash.

"What's The Family?" I asked my Da.

"For sure Kitty you have much to learn. Everybody you've seen at this place is a servant. The house and the farm belong to English people who come here when they want a holiday. They arrive in carriages with special horses to ride and many more servants to look after them and we have to be very polite. Even if we work well they can throw us off the farm if they think we're lazy or cheeky."

"If they bring more servants, why do they need me in the kitchen?"

Da laughed. "English servants don't do dirty work, they just look after The Family. The Irish servants who work in the house have to wait on the servants who come from England. The English servants are the only ones who wait on Family members."

"Will I see any of these people from England?"

"No. You'll be in the scullery and none of them will ever visit that place!"

I didn't much like the way Da said that word *scullery*. I didn't know what it was but it didn't sound pretty. "Do I have to go there Da?"

He nodded. "You're growing up … You need new clothes. You need to be able to look after yourself in case anything happens to me … This is your chance."

"Rather stay with you, Da."

He didn't reply. He looked sad. I said goodnight, rolled myself up in a warm sack and dropped off to sleep.

Two days later Da was told that I was to be ready to go up to the Big House the next morning. The farm overseer would take me up and introduce me to the Cook. I was to be dressed and clean with my hair tied back.

That night Da lit a fire near the shed door, told me to take my clothes off then brought in a big jug of water from the pump and sloshed it all over me. I was frozen. It was the first time I'd ever been wet all over. He took my grubby dress and shift away and took special care to make sure my curly hair was clean. He stood me by the fire, rubbed me all over with a clean sack then he wrapped me in another sack. He wouldn't let me get dressed, I had to sleep in that sack. In the morning he scraped my hair back with a bit of comb he had, then used some string from the sack to tie the curls off my face. Out of another sack he pulled a dress and jacket I'd never worn. They were Lizzie's. There was no shift because Lizzie had been buried in it. The dress was big for me but with the little jacket on top it was warm. I felt very strange and sad to be dressed in Lizzie's clothes. Somehow it seemed wrong when she wasn't there, like stealing. I slipped my feet into my clogs and waited.

Da's friend, Paddy the overseer, arrived. He looked me over and just said "She'll do." I clung to Da but he shook me off. He promised to watch me even if he couldn't come close enough to talk. "We can wave," he said, then he turned his back. A strong, rough hand grabbed mine and off I went to a new life.

Angry Sky

As I left my Da I looked up at the sky. It was a strange colour. It was blue-black with patches of white and little streaks of pale blue. That is the colour of my next patch.

"Sure the rain be coming," said Paddy. "Sky's angry. It's well we finished harvest."

I didn't say anything. It wasn't the sky that was angry, it was me because I'd left my Da. I dragged my feet but a strong hand jerked me and I had to keep up.

At the backdoor I was handed over to the Cook, a very large lady with a very large voice.

"Are you good at cleaning dirty pots?"

How would I know? "Yes ma'am," I said.

"Don't call me that. You call me Cook."

Slowly I discovered that even though everyone had a name it was never used. They had a title. Even I had a title. I was Skivvy, the bottom of the heap.

Cook called a kitchen maid and she took me to the scullery as a footman poured warm water from the stove into a large tin bath. Sally, the maid, told me to take off all my clothes and step into the bath. I put my jacket on a chair and stopped.

"Now your dress," said Sally.

"No, no, no," I cried, "can't take clothes off without Da and Lizzie."

Sally was very kind. She shut the door and crouched down next to me. "Now, now," she said, "no one can see you in here. Sure you'll soon be very pretty."

She started to unbutton my dress. I was so frightened I soiled myself. She wasn't cross. She removed my dress and said she'd wash it. I never saw it again. Feeling very ashamed I stepped into the bath. It was so warm, it was lovely. Sally showed me how to use soap. Making the froth and bubbles was fun.

"Now your hair." She picked up a big pair of scissors.

"Get away," I yelled, but before I knew what was happening she took hold of my hair and cut it back to shoulder length. She washed it and combed out the tangles then wrapped me up in the first towel I had ever seen and dried me all over. I shivered with fright till she showed me my new clothes. There were drawers, a shift and a dress. It was amazing. I'd never seen drawers before, so she had to explain what they were. She also gave me a night shirt and indoor slippers and let me keep Lizzie's jacket.

I started to know what my Da meant when he said I had a lot to learn.

From then on, while ever I worked at the Big House I had regular meals, with meat, about twice a week. I had a bath and hair wash every week and clean clothes too. For the first couple of times Sally showed me where to go for a bath and who to ask for my clean clothes. It was like having Lizzie again. I loved her for that and was sad when some time later she left to get married.

In the scullery I worked with Mary, a kitchen maid. I wasn't a kitchen maid, I was Skivvy or KitKat. I hated that name and I hated Mary. I soon found out that she was lazy and expected me to take the blame for any grime left on a pot. I fixed her by making sure that I checked everything before one of the maids came to collect pots for the kitchen. This worked in my favour. Sally and the other maids were fed up with being given dirty pots. Sally guessed that I was the one cleaning properly.

It didn't take long. After a few weeks Mary was sent packing and I became boss of the scullery but I was still called Skivvy, and I still slept on the bottom shelf of a big cupboard that backed onto the chimneys. It was warm and cosy but all the other maids slept in bedrooms in the attics. They took every chance they had to make fun of me. I was KitKat or just a loud MEOW. My comfort at night time in that strange bed was to fall asleep with Lizzie's jacket in my arms.

Sunday morning was free time so I went to the stile near the stables and Da came to me. I told him all about my job and he told me that he was proud of me in my smart clothes. I didn't tell him the nasty names I was called.

At last The Family arrived. No one told me they had but work doubled over night. At meal times strange maids came in and sat at the kitchen table and were waited on by our own kitchen maids. Cook knew that I had too much to do so Tommy the Boots boy had to help. He worked mostly overnight cleaning the gentry's boots and shoes, then he came into the scullery.

Tommy was a funny, friendly fellow. He told me all about the people who had arrived. There was M'Lady and M'Lord and two young M'Lords who spent their days out riding and chasing foxes and there was a young M'Lady called Louisa who was about my age. She spent her time annoying the maids.

"How?" I asked.

"She jumps into the garden beds, kicks the soil and gets her shoes and skirts dirty, then comes back into the house and goes straight upstairs taking mud everywhere she walks. Sometimes she even climbs onto her bed with her shoes on. She makes a lot of extra work and is rude to all of us. None of us like her."

My days were long. I never got outside the house except for about an hour on Sunday morning when nearly everyone else went to church. Once The Family arrived I was told not to go beyond the kitchen garden so I hoped that Da would come and find me there. When he didn't, Tommy the Boots boy went looking for him.

"He's not there," he told me.

"He must be. Perhaps he's in the fields."

"No Kitty. The shed's empty. No one lives there now."

"Did you look for him?"

"Yes. I found two field workers who remember you and they said he got a new donkey. He went off to be a carter again. He's gone."

I couldn't believe it. My Da had gone away and not told me. That night in bed I wept into Lizzie's jacket, the only thing left to remind me of my family. I didn't tell anyone and I know that Tommy didn't either but in time all the staff found out. The nastiest kitchen maid told me that she knew that he had swapped me for the donkey. I didn't believe her, but when I was told he took most of my wage for the first year I was very upset.

I never saw Da again. Now I look back I think he was always a bit of a gypsy. He enjoyed life on the road. He must have thought I would do better without him.

For at least two years I worked in that scullery. I never saw the Great People. I only knew they'd come or gone by the number of pans to be cleaned. I was supposed to earn nine pounds a year but that was only if The Family was there. When they went back to England, life was fairly easy and pay dropped to five pounds. The Housekeeper kept my money and gave me a shilling a week. There was nothing to spend it on unless a tinker came to the back door selling hair ribbons.

I sometimes worked in the kitchen with the other maids and learnt a few things about cooking and preparing food. I learnt to skin and draw a rabbit but the nastiest job was plucking birds feathers and pulling out their innards. The hardest job was preparing fish caught in the river. All the scales had to be scraped off the skin. It was really tough work. I was in trouble if anyone found scales in the portion on their plate!

On the whole I was happy but I knew that I had to fight for myself if I wanted to get out of the scullery.

One time one of the upstairs maids was sick. I heard about it and asked Cook if I could be given a chance to learn that sort of work. She wasn't pleased but just at that moment Mrs O'Reilly arrived.

"Cook, I shall have to borrow one of the kitchen maids. Polly has gone off sick and Marie just fell down the attic stairs and damaged her arm. I can't work the house two short. Who can you lend me?"

I saw my chance. I did a bob

"Please ma'am, I'd like to try."

Mrs O'Reilly looked astonished. She was the grand lady who talked to me at the harvest party. I had never spoken to her since but I had found out her name and always made sure to do a little bob if she came to talk to Cook while I was there.

"Cook! Who is this? Do I know this bold young person?"

Cook was angry.

"It's Catharine, ma'am. She started with me over two years ago. She should not be putting herself forward. Go to the scullery, miss."

I turned away but I watched what happened.

The women had a long chat. Two other kitchen maids were brought over to meet Mrs O'Reilly but after a quick look she waved them away. Neither of them did a bob, I noticed! One up to me! I was called back into the kitchen.

"Why do you want to work for me, Catharine?"

"Because you're the first person from the house to speak to me. You gave me this job. I like learning new things." I did another bob.

"Good heavens," muttered the Housekeeper, "she can stand up for herself." She glared at me. "Cook tells me you work well but don't talk much. I like the sound of that. Cook, I'll give her a try, just for two weeks then back to the scullery she will come. Catharine, report to me tomorrow before breakfast. Make sure that you are dressed properly for upstairs work and that your hair is very clean. Now go and finish today's jobs and make sure that whatever you do you always give satisfaction."

"Thank you, ma'am," I said and scuttled off to the pots and pans. I wondered about that new word 'satisfaction'. I guessed it must mean that I must do a good job.

I had never been popular in the kitchen. I had no home to visit, no friends that I talked about, no relatives. I didn't even go to church. I was a cast-off who was quiet and kept my gob shut. When I went to get my upstairs uniform I found that I wasn't likely to be popular with the house maids either. They all seemed to think that any scullery maid who (after two years working) was still called "Skivvy" should stay a scullery maid forever. I showed 'em!

The next two weeks were heaven. Upstairs work was easy, just mopping and dusting and making sure that dead flowers were thrown out. The best part was that I got to know what the rest of the house was like. There were big rooms with beautiful chairs and other lovely things like huge pictures of people hanging on the walls. I read the labels on them and found out the names of the people though I can't remember them now. Lord this and Lady that. There were even pictures of horses! Some of them had grander sounding names than the people! The bedrooms were upstairs. The beds were huge.

It was a new world. In all the rooms were great mirrors so I could see all of me! It was interesting and quite a pleasant surprise. My hair was pretty and my dress fitted me.

Most of the furniture was covered by sheets. We had to check that windows were shut and that nothing had been disturbed. Most of the time one of the senior maids was supposed to be with me, but she got tired of that and soon just told me which room to check and what to do. I was very careful to do everything properly and even found a few patches that hadn't been dusted for weeks and brought that to attention. I had to fix it of course but I didn't mind, I was determined never to go back to the Scullery.

At the end of the trial Mrs O'Reilly sent for me.

"Well Catharine, are you ready for the scullery?"

"I'll work anywhere for you, ma'am. I hope I gave satisfaction." I used her big word back at her. "It was a great chance you gave me." I did a bob. I had been practicing in front of the mirrors and knew how to do it better.

Mrs O'Reilly sat back in her chair and laughed.

"Catharine, you amaze me. I think you will do well. You may get to places we can't imagine. Go back to the scullery now but stay in your upstairs uniform."

I did as I was told. In the kitchen, slagging started again.

"Sulky KitKat's in the wrong dress." I didn't say a word.

"Cat's got her tongue" they called. "She's back where she should be, in the Scullery."

I put on a big apron and began to wash pots, thinking all the time about what the Housekeeper had said.

Oh Mrs O'Reilly, could you imagine me here? Could you imagine that I'd end up on the other side of the world. Was it your fault that I did? You gave me the courage to stand up for what I wanted.

Perhaps that's why I now sit in the sun in New South Wales.

No, that's not fair – the reason I'm here is Tolson. Mrs O'Reilly told me the truth about him and I didn't listen to her. The reason I've survived all that happened after I married him is because Mrs O'Reilly in her deep blue dress was always in my thoughts. When I was uncertain what to do I'd sit and think about her. Usually, somehow, she'd tell me which path to choose.

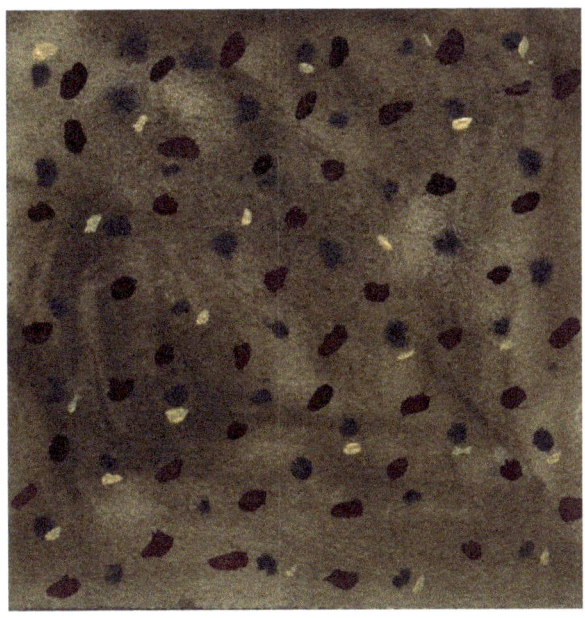

Cinnamon and Gold

For this patch I want material that has lumpy-bumps in it and is a grubby colour. Like grated cinnamon. As I remember those days the grubbiness will fade and gold peep through. I'll use lots of golden embroidery to brighten the patch.

I was now an upstairs house maid. I was the youngest and smallest of them. When I had been on trial I slept on a mattress on the floor of the upstairs broom cupboard with Lizzie's jacket in my arms but now I shared a room and a bed with the next youngest maid. Her name was Bridget.

Bridget saw the jacket and asked what it was. She understood why I wanted to keep it but she thought the knitting was starting to come undone. She folded it carefully, tied one of her hair ribbons around it and suggested that I keep it in a corner of the drawer we shared. I agreed. I would see my precious bundle each time I opened the drawer to find my brush and comb. Bridget had long straight hair that I liked to brush. She liked my curls and would help me comb out the knots. Isn't it funny how all young girls prefer the hair they don't have to whatever's on their heads?

Because we were the youngest we did most of the work but we didn't mind. It was better doing it than hanging around waiting for someone to tell you what to do then turning peevish because we hadn't done it already! Bridget was a good friend. She taught me many things. She bet me that I'd never get a word out of the Butler and that I'd only hear from Mrs O'Reilly if I was in trouble. She asked me why I always talked about Big House instead of Black Grange Manor.

"Is that its name? Never heard it called that," I said. "My Da always talked about Big House."

I wished my Da would come back again. I'd love to tell him all about the inside of Black Grange Manor and my position as an upstairs maid.

I was well into my new life when word came that The Family was to arrive soon.

"Lor 'a mercy," said Bridget, "now we'll have to put up with Miss Louisa. We're sure to be given her room to clean. She makes a right hames (*mess*) of it."

"What do we call her?"

"Just Miss Louisa. She's only a kid so you don't have to bob. Keep that for M'Lord and M'Lady. If the two young M'Lords come, keep out of their way. They like to corner new maids and paw them all over. Ugh!"

To watch their arrival, Bridget took me upstairs onto a landing where we could see the front door. It was very exciting. There were three large carriages and several more horse-drawn vehicles as well as four horses being led by grooms. The first carriage door was opened by the Butler and out stepped a beautiful lady and a fine looking gentleman.

"M'Lord and M'Lady," said Bridget.

M'Lord spoke to the Butler who called a footman forward to the door of the second carriage. Someone was being lifted out and placed in his arms. The person was well wrapped up but Bridget declared it was Miss Louisa.

"What's the craic? She usually jumps out before anyone puts the steps down." A bell jangled loudly. "We're wanted," she said and we raced down the servants' stairs to the back hall.

Mrs O'Reilly was waiting. "Now, girls, Miss Louisa is unwell. Bridget up to her room and make sure everything is in place and fold back the bed. Catharine to the kitchen and get two or three warm bricks to put in the foot of the bed. Try to get this all done before M'Lady arrives."

We moved smartly and were able to have everything in place just as a procession mounted the stairs. M'Lady was in front followed by Miss Louisa in the arms of the footman. We did our best bobs then moved out of the bedroom into the corridor.

Days of fetch and carry began. Mrs O'Reilly was in and out of Miss Louisa's room all the time, instructing Bridget and me what to do. The Doctor came from the village and spent a long time with the patient then in the library meeting with Louisa's parents. We carried hot water into the bedroom and slops and dirty bed linen out. It was smelly and unpleasant. There was no time for chatter. English maids who had arrived with The Family were always in the corridor watching us but they didn't go into the sick girl's room or offer to help. Instead they sent Bridget and me to do whatever the Housekeeper or the Doctor ordered.

Then I was summoned to Mrs O'Reilly's room.

"Have you spoken to Miss Louisa yet, Catharine?"

"Oh no, ma'am. I've been in her room many times but it's hard even to see her. She's never said anything to me though she's peevish about being too hot or too cold. She coughs a lot and vomits and we clean up the mess."

"When you came to work here your father told me that you had cared for your sister when she was sick. Tell me about it."

"Oh, ma'am, it was dreadful. Lizzie couldn't get out of bed. She was so hot that I thought she would burn up and then she was cold. I got into bed with her to try to keep her warm. She wouldn't eat, except a little soup. She got weaker and weaker. It was hard to keep her bed clean but I tried."

"And did you get sick too?"

"No, ma'am. Da said I would, but I didn't … not even for a day."

She dismissed me and I wondered about her questions. Back upstairs I found that Bridget had been sent home because she was poorly and the English maids had left the corridor. I stayed there alone. The Doctor came again to see Miss Louisa then went downstairs to the Library.

I waited and waited until Tommy, who was now a junior footman, came upstairs and told me to come down to the Library.

"You're not in trouble," he said. "Something special's happening"

He took me to the door, opened it and called out "Here is Catharine, M'Lord," and pushed me in. I owe Tommy some thanks for his kind words. It gave me courage.

What a shock I had! In that enormous book-lined room that I'd never been in before, I found M'Lord and M'Lady seated, the Doctor standing in front of the fire and the Butler and Mrs O'Reilly there too. I did a bob then stood with my hands behind my back. Only Mrs O'Reilly spoke:

"Catharine, Miss Louisa is very sick. We need someone to stay with her all the time. The person who does this will eat and sleep in Miss Louisa's room and will have to make sure that she has everything she needs. We want you to do this. The Doctor will visit every day and give you instructions and I will make sure that anything you need is brought up to you. You once said that you would do any job I asked. This is your test. What do you have to say?"

What could I say? Mrs O Reilly was giving me another chance. The Doctor gave me an encouraging smile but no one else even looked at me. I gave the Housekeeper my very best bob and said "I'll do it for you, Mrs O'Reilly." Then I looked at Louisa's parents, a stuffed pair if ever I saw one, did another bob and said "I'll look after her as good as I can."

"Well said," was the Doctor's comment. M'Lord looked at M'Lady who shrugged her shoulders then put a hanky to her eyes but there were no tears in them.

For the first time in my life the Butler spoke to me so I won that bet with Bridget. He said:

"Good work, Catharine. Mrs O'Reilly said you were the right person. Off you go now and she will explain everything to you." I followed the Housekeeper to her private rooms.

The Doctor believed that Louisa might have Typhus, an illness that could be passed on to other people. The Family didn't want the maids from England to catch it because that would endanger the great folk but they needed someone to nurse the sick girl.

The Doctor knew that Typhus had been in my home village when Lizzie died so everyone thought that she probably had it and that for some reason I hadn't been infected. The Doctor thought that I might be immune. That was a new word and Mrs O'Reilly explained it to me.

Mrs O'Reilly asked me what I had heard about Miss Louisa. I told her the truth. I repeated kitchen tattle that Louisa was bad tempered and rude and that none of the staff liked her. She didn't comment but she nodded her head. She warned me that Miss Louisa would not be easy to deal with. She was spoilt by parents who ignored her. They gave her what she wanted so that she kept out of their way. She would not like being left alone with one junior maid her own age. She said that I must stand up for myself and take no notice if Louisa was rude to me. She also told me to be very truthful when the Doctor came and asked me questions.

I kept my thoughts to myself then went to gather all my clothes and things. Tommy arrived with a mattress and followed me upstairs.

Miss Louisa's large room was in two parts. Louisa's bed was in the roomy end where a window opened onto a balcony. Through an archway in one of the walls was a smaller space where my mattress was placed. I was back to sleeping on the floor again with Lizzie's jacket in my arms.

Mrs O'Reilly supervised the arrangements. As Louisa was asleep she told me to watch her and when she woke up, tell her who I was and why I was there. I was to make sure that she drank water from the special jug. Food for both of us would be brought regularly and left outside the door.

Mrs O'Reilly left. I found a small stool which I put near the big windows then I sat down to watch. I felt an eejit (*idiot*) just staring at her. After a while I wandered into the small room where I had seen lots of books, as well as Miss Louisa's toys. I looked at the books and found one with nice pictures that reminded me of the pictures I'd seen when I went to school. I borrowed *Bible Stories* and went back to the stool.

I looked at all the pictures then went back to the beginning to see what I could read. I was very slow. I found it easier to speak the words aloud. It was such fun that I forgot why I was there.

"Who are you? What are you doing? How dare you steal my book."

I leapt to my feet, dropped the book and went to Louisa's bedside. She was half sitting up. Her hair was soaking wet and her skin bright pink. She reminded me of Lizzie.

"Oh Miss," I said, "do lie down again and I'll get you a drink."

"Who are you?" she cried again as she sank back onto the

pillows.

"I'm your nurse. I'll be with you all the time."

"I don't want you. I hate the way you talk. You're a lazy, dumb Irish servant and I don't want you in my room." Louisa began to cough. I thought she might vomit so I picked up a bowl. She saw what I had done. "How dare you!" she yelled. "Get away. I won't have you near me." It was too much for her. What I expected happened but I managed to catch the fluid in the bowl then with a clean cloth I wiped her face.

She was exhausted and slumped back onto the pillows. I straightened her bed clothes, put the smelly bowl outside the door and sat on my stool. Louisa lay with her eyes half closed watching me.

"What's your name?"

"Catharine."

"Where did you come from?"

"I work here. I'm an upstairs maid. I used to work in the scullery …" (foolish me!)

"I knew it. You're a dirty, rotten little skivvy. I won't have you near me. Pull that bell and get my mother here."

I did as I was told and wondered who would answer the bell. In sailed Mrs O'Reilly.

"Well, Miss Louisa, I see that you have met Catharine. She is one of our best upstairs maids and the Doctor asked me to allow her to work in your room as your nurse. While you are ill you need someone here with you and Catharine it is. Your parents agreed with the Doctor."

"Where is mother? I want her to come and see me."

"Not possible, Miss Louisa. The Doctor doesn't want your mother or father picking up this illness. Catharine will be here and I shall visit from time to time. Now I must go. There is much to do when Your Family arrives." With that she stalked out of the room.

As she listened to the Housekeeper, Louisa's eyes got bigger and bigger. She screwed up her face and started to make a strange noise. I thought she was crying but then I decided that she was really laughing. I couldn't make it out. I thought I'd leave her alone and go back to my stool. I wanted to think about Mrs O'Reilly calling me 'one of our best upstairs maids'. Did she really think that?

After a little while the noise from the bed stopped. Louisa seemed to be asleep so I picked up the book.

"Put it down. How dare you. You can't read anyway. My parents are scared of catching something from me. What about you? Aren't you scared? No one seems to care if you get ill. We'll probably both die." I knew she might well be right but I said nothing. Instead I began to read aloud the words I had already found. I stumbled over one and from the bed I heard how to say it.

"Thank you, Miss," I said and went on reading. Shortly after Louisa fell asleep.

I read until there was no more light coming through the window then I put the book away and checked the sick girl. She was sweating a lot and throwing the covers off. Although she fought me, I just kept putting them back as gently as I could. There was a knock at the door. By the time I opened it there was no one to see but on the little table outside was a tray with two bowls of soup and some crusty bread. The crockery and cutlery on the tray made it clear which bowl was mine. Kitchen ware is quite different from dining room ware. I brought the tray in and had mine straight away. In all the excitement I hadn't eaten anything since breakfast.

"Miss Louisa," I whispered, "have some soup." I waved a spoonful near her hoping the smell would wake her up. She didn't stir. I drew the curtains, lit a lamp then settled down to see what might happen. Only once that night did she waken and call for a drink. I managed to get her to swallow a little water then she slept again. I found a comfy chair, pulled it over near the bed, curled up in it and slept too.

For many days I thought Louisa would die. I had to change her nightdress and wash her and change the bed clothes. She was sweating so much that her whole bed was damp. I told the Doctor and he arranged for Tommy to light a fire in the room. He gave instructions that only the best coal, called anthracite, was to be used. He said it would make less dust than ordinary coal and that dust was bad for Louisa's cough. Tommy told me how Paddy from the farm, spent a whole day travelling to the mine to get it. Tommy brought up a scuttle full every morning so that I was able to keep the fire going. Mrs O'Reilly came to the door many times each day to question me and to make sure that I had everything I needed.

The trays that came up from the kitchen always had plenty of food and mine was the same as hers but Louisa wouldn't take any at all. When she woke up she didn't know me. She talked nonsense. The Doctor said everything was caused by the illness. He came once or even twice a day. The only thing I got into her mouth was plain water and the Doctor said that the more she had the better she would be. I thought that the more she had the more she sweated but what did I know? Perhaps he wanted her to sweat. I did what he told me.

It was lonely with no one to talk to. I wished Louisa would wake up and abuse me. It'd be good to give her a bit of cheek. I read three books during that time. They were all tales for children but I enjoyed them. I also opened the little box that the farmer's wife had given me. It contained some scraps of material and a selection of needles and threads. I can practise now, I thought. Sewing was a great change from trying to untangle words.

Mrs O'Reilly found me busy one day and asked to see my work. She said it was good and sent me up some napkins to darn. With them was a note from Bridget. "I'm back at work. I'm better now. Hope I can help you soon." That was good news.

At last Louisa woke up properly. She lay looking about the room and at last she looked at me.

"I'm glad you're sitting in the chair. It's comfier than the stool."
I hadn't used that stool since my first day as her nurse. She had no idea how long she had been ill.

"Is your name Catharine?"

"Yes, Miss."

"I thought I had dreamed it but you seem to be real. You do talk funny with your Irish words. Who works with you?"

"I'm alone, Miss."

"Who helps you when you give me water?"

"Just me."

"You're small but you must be very strong and you're really gentle. Can I have a drink?"

For once she held the glass in her hand though she nearly spilt it. She was very weak. She smiled then went back to sleep.

When Mrs O'Reilly came I told her of the change. Bridget carried up the next meal. For the first time there was a difference between the two meals. Bridget waited to speak to me and said that I was to leave what Miss Louisa didn't eat or drink on the tray, including the very small glass of wine. I suppose they were worried that I'd steal it! It made me cross. Next time the Doctor came he explained. They needed to measure how much Miss Louisa was able to eat and drink.

It was a long time before Louisa was able to get out of bed. M'Lady came in one day but she didn't stay long. She just looked at her daughter and told me to do a better job with the hairbrush. She looked out the window, complained about the rain and left. She was hard. The next morning she returned.

"Louisa, your father is needed in London. We are leaving tomorrow but the Doctor says you are not to travel yet. Don't argue with me, we must listen to the Doctor. I shall leave Rebecca, my junior maid, to be your companion and maid. Catharine can go back to her normal duties."

Louisa sat straight up in bed.

"No she can't," she screamed. "She's the only one I want helping me."

"Don't be ridiculous, child. She is a house maid, not a lady's maid. She wouldn't know how to care for your clothes and her Irish speech is starting to affect you. Rebecca will replace her."

Louisa screamed then picked up a glass of water and threw it at her mother. Luckily she missed!

"I won't have Rebecca! I hate her and she hates me. She can't sew and Catharine has already mended nightdresses for me. Her needlework is better than mine. You just want to get away from here and from me. You're mean and unfair." She stopped talking, had a severe coughing fit then buried her head under the pillow and began to cry. M'Lady walked out.

Before long Mrs O'Reilly appeared. "Well, Catharine, it looks as if you will go on working for Miss Louisa for some time."

Louisa's head appeared from under the covers.

"You mean I won, Mrs O'Reilly?"

The Housekeeper didn't answer. She had on her business face.

"Your parents leave early tomorrow morning. Rebecca goes with them. Your brothers left yesterday. From now on you will have to rely on the Doctor and me and Catharine. When you are quite well, arrangements will be made for you to go home."

Louisa smiled. "Thank you," she said and began to weep quietly.

By now the colour of my patch has changed completely. The golden part of my life began. We became friends. We worked out that she was at least a year older than me. I stopped calling her Miss and just called her Louisa. She called me Cathie. She laughed at the way I talked and sometimes copied me, but I had more fun copying her. Slowly, slowly, I began to alter how I spoke.

In the following months I got to know her, the good and the bad bits. I learnt a lot from her, even when she was cruel to me. She opened my eyes to books and to beauty and to what changes the way people behave. She was like a golden thread that grew into my mind. Sometimes the gold was brilliant like bright metal and sometimes it was black and ugly. Both sides of Louisa were useful lessons.

Louisa helped me with my reading. She stopped me using what she called 'baby books' and made me try some books she had brought with her from London. They were very different. They were long stories about grown-up people living grand lives in England. One was called *Northanger Abbey* and it was written by a lady whose first name was Jane, like my second name. It was a good book. I liked to pretend that the lady in it was like me – young and not up-to-date with how to behave. I was fooling myself of course. I lived in a totally different world and could never join hers.

Louisa often pretended that she was too tired to read and would ask me to read to her. She was gentle and patient and always explained what new words meant and how to say them. I tucked them all into my head. I wanted to be able to read and speak properly.

One morning Louisa asked me about the little bundle I kept under my pillow. Very carefully I placed Lizzie' jacket on the table and told her its story.

"Cathie, that is such a sad story. No wonder you want to have something to remember her by but Bridget is right. It will fall to pieces soon because the knitting is coming undone and the moths have been eating it."

"Yes, Miss, but I loved Lizzie so," I began to cry.

"Don't cry. Let's think about it for a minute … is there a button on it?"

"Yes, Miss." Carefully I turned the jacket round and as I did one of the sleeves pulled right away. "Oh, Miss, look what's happened."

"Never mind … look at that lovely wooden button." Louisa picked it up and found that the wool holding it was broken. "You must never lose this button, Cathie. It will last forever. I will make you a little bag to keep it in."

True to her word, Louisa used one of her handkerchiefs to make a bag with a draw string at the top. The button had a safe home. Before long I had to throw the jacket away but the button is with me still.

Louisa watched my progress with sewing. She had some work of her own, a very pretty sampler with lots of different colours and designs that she made up herself. She taught me how to do the fancy stitches that she used and in the end I did more work on her sampler than she did herself.

Now that Louisa was no longer infectious Bridget often helped me with my work. We changed the curtains and slowly cleaned everything in Miss Louisa's room. My mattress was shifted and I was back sharing with Bridget. When Louisa was able to stay out of bed we helped her put on a pretty dress and then we'd take her down stairs. At first we had to hold her on both sides but soon she could manage with just one of us and at last the day came when she didn't need our help at all.

At first we had to stay in the house. We were allowed in the Breakfast Room and the Library but we were not allowed to use M'Lord's desk. We could sit near the fire and Louisa could choose books from that end of the room. I often wondered about the books that we weren't allowed to touch. It was several years before I was able to peek at them. Some of them were full of numbers and lists but some had really rude pictures of people in them. I never told Louisa about that but I suspect she knew.

Whenever there was a dry day we ventured into the garden, into the sun but out of the wind. She would read or sew or doze while I did house sewing. Mrs O'Reilly kept an eye on us but while we kept her rules there were no problems. I wondered how long it would be before Louisa would be sent home but I never asked about that. I just waited.

I loved being in the gardens. They were beautiful. Long sweeping lawns and flower beds that were changed regularly so there was nearly always something in bloom. The gardeners were always busy.

One day the chief gardener was working near us. Louisa watched as he planted new flowers.

"How beautiful they are," she said. He looked surprised.

She blushed. "I know I have often trampled on your work. It was wrong of me. I'll never do it again."

"Thank'ee, Miss." He smiled and moved away. Gossip went round the Manor very quickly –

"She's not the brat she used to be!"

Fading Gold

For this patch I'll look for a piece of fawn material and on it embroider a setting sun.

Louisa stayed at Black Grange Manor till her parents returned the next year. Even then I was permitted to remain her personal servant. Although they never spoke to me, her parents accepted that I would spend most of the day with her.

We often sat in the garden and when Louisa was able to ride again, I had fun watching her. She sometimes said that she wanted me to be able to ride with her but she never mentioned that idea to her brother, who usually accompanied her. It was just blarney.

She also learnt to drive a small pony cart and then she let me go with her when she drove it around the Manor Park or to church. Most of the staff went to the Catholic church but Louisa went to the English church. I'd never been to any church before so I was curious. When she went, I went. I enjoyed the hymns but found the parson's talk boring and didn't understand a lot of it but it was a good place to practise reading.

Mostly we stayed in the grounds of the Manor. Sometimes Louisa would stop the pony cart in a wooded area and we'd climb down and share a small picnic basket that Mrs O'Reilly had prepared for us. I really enjoyed it and thought it would go on forever. How naive I was.

(Naive is a great word. I learnt it a long time later. Louisa taught me.

"You're SO naive!" she yelled. "You think you know me! You don't and you can't. We are different!"

I still didn't know what that new word meant and I certainly couldn't spell it but I got the general idea.)

Before she left to go back to London, Louisa gave me permission to read any of the books in her room. She also left me several of her old dresses. So there'd be no suggestion that I had stolen them, she discussed her plan with Mrs O'Reilly. That good woman actually sat with us while Louisa pulled things out for me to try. I only kept dresses that were a bit too big for me and that were not too grand for a servant. Mrs O'Reilly saw to that and she was right. It doesn't do for a servant to be too fancy in her dress. It makes the other servants jealous and outsiders think you're further up the social scale than you are! Getting your 'place' just right is an important trick.

Speech is also important. Louisa and I had a game of copying each other but her purpose was really to rub the rough edges off my broad Irish accent, not to start adopting it herself. I was a good mimic. I dropped some expressions I had learnt from my Da and slowed my speech. The result was noticed by the rest of the staff. I still had the Irish lilt in my voice but my accent was much easier to understand.

On the day The Family left, Louisa kissed me on both cheeks

and thanked me for being a good nurse and friend. She said that apart from Mrs O'Reilly I was the only person she trusted at Black Grange Manor. I was surprised to be likened to someone as important as the Housekeeper. I didn't tell Bridget. I didn't want to give gossips an excuse to say I had ideas above my station.

Once again I was back to being a full-time housemaid. I enjoyed it, especially having fun with Bridget. Often she invited me to come with her on Sunday when she visited her family. I enjoyed a bit of family life but it made me sad as well. Too many memories of things best forgotten.

Mrs O'Reilly used me more and more for needlework. I did a lot of darning of household linen and she encouraged me to complete two pieces of embroidery Louisa had left behind. I also filled in part of a large piece of canvas tapestry M'Lady had been doing. I was told to work only on the bits that the Housekeeper knew M'Lady didn't like doing. I thought it was a good Irish joke that she'd never know the person she despised most was the person who helped her.

It was more than two years before Miss Louisa returned to Ireland. I nearly didn't recognise her. She was much taller and she had a real figure. I only came up to her shoulder and I was flat as a board! I watched her alight from the carriage and expected that she wouldn't want to know me.

I was wrong. I became her personal maid again. I was no longer her main companion but I was the person who made her lazy life easy and smooth. I was also the person she shared some secrets with and made sure she could get in and out of the house unseen. Oh yes, there was a young man involved. She knew him in London and his family owned an estate near the Manor. He was a friend of her brothers and had ignored Louisa for years but now he was finding her interesting – much more interesting than either of her big brothers.

Louisa took a liking to the conservatory where the gardener kept all the delicate indoor plants. We went there mid-morning with a book and our needlework. It was quite private. Her beau, Mr George, came most days. He had a beautiful horse. He always arrived with his groom, a fellow much the same age as himself, called Tolson who looked after the horses until the young pair went off for a ride. Tolson was supposed to go with them but always lagged behind. He told me he was instructed to keep out of sight and was paid to come so far into the trees and then stop. That meant, of course, that Louisa and George might have gone anywhere or done anything. I'm sure they did!

If Louisa ordered tea for George in the conservatory, I took Tolson to the kitchen. He was a great entertainer. Even Cook enjoyed his nonsense. He was good-humoured, keeping everyone in the kitchen laughing, as he told tales about life in London and about his successes as a jockey in big races. He quite captured my interest. I thought he was rather special. I had no way of knowing what a liar he was. He told me that I was special. He told me that his master approved of me and hoped that I'd always be Louisa's maid. He hinted that when the couple married I would be able to remain with Louisa. I swallowed it all. Naive again!

Louisa was not quite nineteen years old. George was several years older. She told me that, when she went back to London, she expected a great party for her birthday, so that her engagement to George could be made public. Of course I asked her if she loved George. Her answer came with a standard Louisa snarl:

"I'll marry anyone if it gets me away from this family."

That wasn't the answer I expected. Jane Austin's books always linked love with marriage.

"Will you visit Ireland when you're married?"

"I suppose so. George's family own an estate near here."

"Good," I said. "I can still work for you when you're not in England."

Louisa didn't reply. She just smiled and went back to the book she was reading.

Not many days later, while a nervous Louisa hid in her room, there was a long, loud row in the Library. I'm not sure who was there. Word came out that trunks were to be packed for immediate departure. I joined Louisa in her room and started packing. She said nothing – just watched me work. I chatted about her birthday party but she didn't reply. She was very quiet. Usually she was excited when she was on her way back to London but this time she seemed scared.

"Which of my books do you most enjoy reading?" she asked

"My favourite is *Northanger Abbey*."

"Why? I think it's a bit silly."

"For sure, Louisa, it's the first you helped me with. It 'minds me of when we became friends."

"Huh," was her reply. "What else?"

"Well … I think the creepy one is great!"

"You mean *Frankenstein?*"

"Yes."

"Well that's a surprise. If you're sure, you can have them both to remember me by." She took them off the shelf and inside each wrote *For Catharine, my friend*.

A little later an English maid came to the door and said, "M'Lady is waiting."

Louisa sailed out the door, down the stairs and into the waiting carriage. She didn't wave. She didn't look back. I felt sure there was trouble coming her way.

Not for me though. I was a housemaid again. Bridget was still my friend and we had lots of news to share. The best bit was that she and Tommy the Footman were to be married. That was grand news, they'd been walking out for months. I would miss her and to celebrate her friendship I bought her several emerald green hair ribbons, the colour she loved.

Bridget told me a lot of gossip about Miss Louisa's young man.

People were saying that he was a gambler and wanted to marry Miss Louisa for her money. It was said that he didn't even own the horse he used to ride. I ignored most of the gossip and didn't believe it until the day I chanced to meet Mrs O'Reilly in the garden. I said good morning and then felt brave enough to ask if Miss Louisa was going to marry Mr George.

"Ah, Catharine, what did she tell you?"

"That there was to be a party soon and that her parents would tell people about the marriage plans."

"Well, Catharine, you may as well know the truth. Miss Louisa is married. There was no party. Instead the wedding took place as soon as The Family arrived back in London. Your time as a lady's maid is over. She will not live here again."

I was very disappointed so I told Bridget about it.

"Miss Louisa didn't have the big party ... I wonder why. She'll be cross about it," I said.

Bridget looked very knowing. "I bet there's a wee one on the way."

The suggestion made me cross. I walked away from Bridget and went into Louisa's room to think. The more I thought, the more I suspected that Bridget might be right. Louisa had been very quiet and secretive ever since the time her parents went off to Dublin for a few days and she was allowed to remain at home with her brother Thomas. Mr George visited every day and stayed some nights after he and Thomas got drunk over a game of cards. During the day she and Mr George were never apart; Thomas was never in the house and I was told that I wasn't needed. Most of the time I had no idea where she was.

I decided that if I heard she was living at Mr. George's home, I would make it my business to visit.

I saw her sooner than I expected.

I often went to the English church on Sundays. Louisa had taken me there. I still didn't understand much about the service but the hymns were fun. I had a good clear voice and liked to join in. Some of the other people said they liked to hear me sing! While the parson prayed and preached I read bits and pieces of the prayer book or looked around at the fashions. One Sunday I saw that there was a lady sitting in a front pew behind Miss Louisa's old pew. She was by herself. I moved until I could catch sight of her face around the bonnet brim. It was Louisa!

At the end of the Service I sat in my place and waited for her to leave. She didn't move until the church was nearly empty. When she saw me she looked shocked and turned her head.

"Miss Louisa," I said, "don't you know me?"

"Of course. Why are you here?" She sounded very cross.

"I often come. 'Twas a surprise I got when I saw you. Where's Mr George?"

"In London." Louisa slumped into a pew and hid her face.

The parson came back into the church and stopped to speak to Louisa but she waved him away. Once we were alone, we moved outside to wait for her carriage.

As she walked she leant on my arm just as she had done when I looked after her all those years ago. I could see that she wasn't well. At last she looked at me properly.

"I don't want to talk to you again. My life is difficult. My husband has told me to have nothing to do with anyone from Black Grange Manor. I cannot meet you again. If you ever see me you must turn away."

"Louisa, what nonsense. You aren't well, you need someone to care for you. I'll come and work at your new home."

"It's true – I'm not well, but I can't have you anywhere near me."

"Yes you can! I'll hand in my notice and work for you."

"No, no, no, " she screamed. "You're SO naive! You think you know me! You don't and you can't. We are different. NEVER, call me Louisa again. Never, never speak to me again."

I was shocked. I could hear horses and round the corner came a small carriage driven by Tolson.

"Sorry I'm late, ma'am." He jumped down and helped Louisa into it. She looked at me, shook her head then turned away. Tolson winked at me before turning the carriage and setting off at a fair pace for her home.

When I got back to the Manor I told Cook I didn't feel like eating and went up to my room. I didn't want to talk to anyone. Bridget arrived but I told her that I wasn't well. She left me alone. Next time I saw her she told me that Mrs O'Reilly wanted to see me. In the Housekeeper's room I heard the rest of the story.

"Was Miss Louisa in church today?" she asked.

I burst into tears and told her that Louisa didn't want to know me. Mrs O'Reilly sighed.

"You looked after that young woman for years. I think you deserve to know the truth but you are never to share it with anyone. Louisa is quite unwell. She is expecting a baby and it is not going smoothly."

"Why? What's wrong?"

"I don't know. The London Doctor suggested that she rest. Her husband decided that she should come here until the baby is born."

"Why isn't Mr George with her then? Who's caring for her?"

"Men usually keep clear when a baby's coming. They aren't interested … Louisa wrote and asked me to release you to be her maid but when her husband and parents found out there was a row. I was given strict instructions to keep you here and she was told she must have nothing to do with any of us."

We sat in silence for a minute or two then I blurted out something I'd been thinking about for years:

"Ma'am, when you first asked me to nurse Louisa I thought it was right for me to be chosen for the job. Later I decided it showed how little her parents cared. They weren't much worried about Louisa and not at all worried about me. They wouldn't have cared if either of us went the same way as my Lizzie … If I had died, who would have noticed or cared?"

"I would have, Catharine." There were tears in her eyes as Mrs O'Reilly spoke. "The Doctor didn't really believe that Louisa had Typhus. I let him persuade me that you would be safe. Had anything happened to you, I would have left my position in this House the day you were buried."

I knew that she was speaking the truth so I told her something I had never reported from that sick-room.

"You know, Louisa knew that we might both die. It was one of the first things she ever said to me. She more or less said that we were both of no importance."

By now we were both in tears. Mrs O'Reilly rang for a pot of tea and we did our best to look natural when Bridget arrived with the tray. I was still curious about several other things.

"Who came from London with Louisa?"

"Only her personal maid and Tolson."

"She must be frightened and lonely."

"That may well be true, Catharine … Just you remember that nobody from this house can do anything to help her."

"If Mr George isn't here, why is Tolson?"

"I don't know. Mr George seems to trust him."

"Is he a spy?"

"Possibly."

"Does Louisa hate me?"

"No."

"Does Mr George hate me"?

"Possibly. He believes that you encouraged Louisa to pursue him and now he's sorry that he married her. He is not interested in her or the baby. Her parents blame you for not telling them that Louisa and Mr George were seeing so much of each other and Mr George said that he would never trust you as a house servant."

How unfair can people be? Parents who never wanted to know

where their daughter was. Brothers who encouraged their friend to get to know their sister but never stayed around when he visited. A suitor who paid his groom to keep out of the way.

I let Mrs O'Reilly know that I thought the whole thing was disgraceful. "I suppose I'll lose my job now!"

She didn't answer straight away but she looked very thoughtful.

"No one could complain about your work," she said, "but your position is odd. If M'Lady turns against you then I can't do much to help. I couldn't even give you a reference. You know that she never approved of you spending so much time with Louisa. She put up with it to keep Louisa happy. You were very good at that job …
… Would you be interested in more nursing?"

I stared at her. "What do you mean?"

"My sister lives in Dublin. She works for a family with a very young child. The child is poorly. They are looking for someone to assist with her care."

"What's wrong with her?"

"Nothing that has a name. She was born very small and weak and she is very slow to grow. She is now four years old and can only walk a little. If you took the job you would live in Dublin and never come back here. You would have to make your own way … Think about it."

I thought about it all week. There was no-one I could talk to. I went to church the next Sunday just to see if Louisa came. She had and Tolson was standing outside. He stood in my way. "Be careful," he said. "Miss Louisa is watched all the time. Her life is difficult. My master's cruel … I knew he was hard on horses but he is harder on his wife. He will hurt you too if he wants to."

"Is he here now?"

"No. He has spies."

"Like you?" I said.

"No! Not this time. I tell him nothing but if he questions me … lying ain't easy."

I turned my back on him and crept into the back pew of the church where I spent my time thinking about Mrs O'Reilly's words. I left before the end of the service so that I would not be seen by Louisa or her maid and hurried home. I saw the Housekeeper and told her what had happened. I asked if it would be possible to visit Dublin and find out more about the little girl. I had never had a holiday so she said she would write to her sister and tell her about my nursing experiences, then she would give me a week's holiday to go and meet the family.

So it happened, and before the month was out I left Kilkenny for good with the back wages that had been kept for me in my purse.

On the day before I left Mrs O'Reilly gave me an excellent reference and we had a long talk. She said something that I thought rather strange at the time but it stuck in my head and helped me more than once:

"You may be small in stature, Catharine, but you are strong in your mind and your body. Always think tall and hold your head high, especially when you are dealing with awkward people."

Four Stripes

There are four parts to this patch and the first will be primrose yellow, a dear little girl's favourite colour.

Lucy was a darlin'. She was tiny and not at all strong but she was happy and friendly. She spent a lot of time at the window in a chair so I set out to see if I could get her up and about. I asked if she could have a kitten and she was soon very interested watching it play. That encouraged her to move more but she tired quickly.

Her parents' stripe is a richer old-gold colour, a bit like mustard. They were a very pleasant elderly couple, Lucy being their only child. The Doctor visited regularly and he told me that Lucy must not be allowed to catch cold but that taking her for walks outside would be good, as long as she was always warm and cosy. I had a push-chair for her and, when spring came, every fine day we went out to the park near the river to watch the ducks.

One summery day I saw a man watching us. He approached the bench I was sitting on and I recognised Tolson. He asked if he could sit with me and we exchanged news, including the fact that Miss Louisa's baby was a boy and that they had returned to London. He said he had been dismissed when Mr George found out that I had met and talked to Louisa. He had found another job with a man who trained racing horses and frequently travelled between London and Dublin. He was interested to know that I was living in Dublin and said that he would contact me whenever he was here.

The third stripe is darker – with the colour and shine of well-polished brown boots.

Over the next year I saw him several times. I told the Housekeeper, and she said that he could come to the servant's door if he wanted to meet me. She made it clear that Lucy came first and that I must not neglect her.

As if I would! The child was a delight. She was like the doll I never had but I began to wonder if she would reach adulthood.

Because of his occasional visits to Dublin, Tolson became part of my life.

The housekeeper told her sister so I soon had a letter from Mrs O'Reilly. She said Tolson was not a reliable fellow. He had been sacked by Mr George's family because he had injured two horses and he was known to be a gambler with more debts than winnings. These were the same things that had been said about Mr George in the past. Which of these men abused horses and gambled? Was it both or was it neither?

I asked Tolson if the story about the injured horses was true. He told me a long yarn and of course in his telling Mr George was the one who had injured the horses and Tolson had been blamed. I was sure Mr George had a bad temper so I accepted that the Tolson version of the tale was true.

I watched for signs of gambling but never saw anything to make me suspicious. He always had ready cash to take me for an outing and his clothes and boots were clean and smart. He seemed reliable to a naive fool like me.

Little Lucy grew weaker. Time came when she rarely left her bed. The Doctor shook his head and the Mistress spent most of her days sitting with me in the nursery. The Master visited often and I spent a lot of time working on a patch-work quilt, made from little garments that the child no longer wore.

Lucy died a few weeks after her sixth birthday. Her parents and the Doctor and I were all with her. She had eaten a little food and then settled herself on her pillow. She looked around at us all with her beautiful smile then closed her eyes in sleep. It wasn't sleep anymore. She had slipped away.

I helped my Mistress prepare the delicate body and asked if I could wrap Lucy in the quilt that I had made. She said she would rather I kept it to remember the fun the little girl had, choosing which patches to put in it. I still have some pieces of that quilt, though most of it went into the ground with another child.

For many days the house was full of mourning. Even after the funeral, the Mistress spent most of her time in the nursery. Once I'd cleaned it, there was little for me to do. The Housekeeper kept me busy with preparations for callers but after a few weeks that came to an end as well. I knew that I'd have to think about another job. There was nothing for me any longer in that sad household.

Now it is time for the fourth stripe. I will choose a piece of many coloured striped material. My life was about to change in so many different ways, the greatest being that quite suddenly I was an independent adult, totally responsible for my future.

Tolson had been very respectful during Lucy's final months. He only visited once but he wrote me a letter (his spelling was worse than mine!) and told me that he thought we should get married. He planned to live in England and he said there would be lots of jobs for me there. I wondered how he knew but I accepted it.

I talked to the Housekeeper and I talked to the few people I had come to know since I arrived in Dublin. Jobs were not easy to find in that city and local householders looked for Catholic servants. I went to a hospital run by Catholic Nuns to see if I could become a nurse. I was told that they'd employ me as a skivvy, though if I became a Catholic they might train me to assist with nursing. I didn't fancy any of that. I wasn't much for any church but at least at the English church I understood what was being said. Bridget once took me to a Catholic service where I found they used a different language altogether. What was the point of that? No, that wasn't for me. I gave up on a nursing career.

My employment was about to end. I had to make a decision. I spent a day off with Tolson and found him full of plans. He was going into a new job in England with a horse breeder and trainer who would provide us with a cottage. It was in the country and there were grand homes nearby that were always looking for staff. He was confident that I'd find a position, especially as I had good references. He had to leave the next week.

I believed him. To be truthful it sounded more exciting than anything I could imagine in Dublin.

Did I want to get married? Yes I did. I'd like to have children one day. He knew I had no relatives and didn't care. Being with him was like being with Bridget. He was friendly and easy. I said I'd marry him and he agreed to arrange for our wedding and for tickets on the ship that crossed the Irish Sea. Of course I gave him most of my little hoard of money to help pay for the parson and those tickets. Was I naive or just plain stupid?

Did I love him? No. I didn't know what love meant. I was taken in by his blarney and the excitement of starting a new and unknown life.

I announced my plans to the Mistress. She and the Master gave me a reference. The Housekeeper gave me another and agreed to come to the wedding as my witness. Within a week I was Catharine Jane Tolson, with a narrow gold ring on my left hand and a certificate that Tolson kept – that I never saw again.

The next day I had my first experience of ship life, so the stitching that joins the four stripes together is greeny-blue, the colour of the water we sailed across on a balmy day with wind to fill the sails but not enough to rock the boat.

Destructive Darkness

What is the colour of hatred? I don't know but I do know this will be an ugly patch. It will be made of the roughest cloth I can find. It will be covered with the letter X. My little bit of schooling taught me that anything wrong is rewarded with an X. I will cover this patch again and again with Xs so that in the end the cloth will disappear and anyone looking at it will see that everything that happened was wrong.

Tolson was everything Mrs O'Reilly said and lots more. He was cruel. He was violent. He was dishonest. He was lazy. He was a liar. He gambled or drank every penny he had (including mine) then pawned my wedding ring. Why did he marry me? Sometimes I thought it was because he, a very short man, found that I was shorter still! I was someone he could look down on. The real reason was probably money. I suspect he believed I would always earn more than he could. I would get the money he craved that would keep him in food and beer.

Was I ever happy? For the first few days after the wedding we were on the move all the time. He was attentive, kissed me once and pawed me a bit but said that he thought we should wait till we were in our home to celebrate being wed. I didn't mind. Although we'd spent time together over a number of years we had never been sweethearts. I wasn't in any hurry for him to claim his rights. Until we got to his job he was as I had always seen him – amusing and friendly. He never stopped saying that together we'd be well off, we'd be good partners. I believed him and enjoyed his company.

While we were on the ship he let slip that during a previous job spread between Ireland and England, he had been employed by the ship's owner. At the time he told me he managed horse transport for a trainer. Really he was always just a stable hand.

We got to Epsom where, for the first time, I saw him in the company of other men. His manner changed overnight. He knew the other workers and spent his free time with them at the closest pub. He often didn't come home at night. In my hearing he told the men that I was an Irish slut not good for anything, even in bed. That was meant to be an insult but as he'd never shared a bed with me I didn't much care what he said. I began to wonder if I had ever known him. When he did spend a night at home he was a drunken mess and just slept where he dropped, leaving me alone. That was a relief. I didn't want to have a child unless things improved.

We were living near the race track at Epsom. His employer wasn't a horse breeder, he wasn't even a trainer. This was the second lie I discovered. The boss had a string of stables and he rented them out to breeders. Tolson had to clean the stables as well as help exercise the horses. He was a stable-hand and as such his pay was poor. The two-room cottage we had was part of his pay. When he discovered that, he told me to look for a live-in job. He planned to let out floor space to his drunken mates in return for free booze.

Close by, in a village called Walton-on-the-Hill, there were some big houses and I went to all of them looking for work. As soon as they knew my name they lost interest. Tolson had worked in the area before. Even my references weren't good enough to overcome my husband's name. I learnt that he'd been a failure as a jockey (another lie), was suspected of theft and not trusted. Not surprisingly they weren't in a hurry to trust me either.

When I talked to Housekeepers about employment I always mentioned my needlework experience and in the end that led to work in two or three houses. If there was a lot of darning to be done I'd be given a day's work and put into a small room near the Housekeeper. It was piece-work and I was paid for what I did. If the light was bad and I could only work for an hour or two then that is what I did. If it was high summer I might sew for eight or nine hours at a time. I was never encouraged to talk to the other staff and it was clear that I would never be given anything more permanent. I was, however, given a decent midday meal. Tolson got a meal at the stables.

Tolson hated me for my failure to get a live-in position. He wanted my earnings not my company. He was keen to have the cottage to himself while I lived elsewhere and got an income he could claim. He took my earnings then hit me, taking care not to damage my hands or bruise my face. He was a sadistic brute.

'Sadistic' is another good word. I learnt that later, during my long sea voyage, but I knew straight away that it was made for Tolson.

I was lucky that my skills with the needle became known. The stable boss had two little girls. I began to sew for them and their mother. Out of that we were lent a good lamp for our cottage so I could sew at night and earn more.

Time passed and I began to wonder how best to get out of the mess I was in. I had no money and was in a strange country. Of course Tolson solved the problem.

On race days he was a strapper, guarding the runners before

leading them to the jockeys. He hated the jockeys and had tricks to make the horses dance and dodge when the jockey was trying to get into the saddle. The jockeys returned his hatred and were always looking for opportunities to flick him with the whip.

The end came when he got drunk on the day of a really important race. He led a horse into an iron post causing it to cut its leg, then told the owner that the jockey had done it. The owner didn't believe that story and threatened my stupid husband with a horsewhipping if he ever went near a horse again. The stable boss was furious. He ordered us to pack up and get out. We lost our home and our income. What next?

Tolson insisted that we go to London. We walked. He put me into a dirty room at the top of a dirty rooming house and took himself off to see a friend. He came back the next day very puffed up, changed his jacket and told me to smarten up because it was a 'dead cert' he'd be back soon with a job for both of us.

By now I knew that Tolson never thought much before he raced off to chase a 'dead cert'. As a gambler he always lost. The fool had found out that one of Mr. George's friends was looking for a groom. What he didn't find out was that Mr George knew about Epsom. He had been there and knew the man who owned the injured horse, a horse so badly hurt it had been put down. Mr George had told all his friends about the incident and that Tolson, his ex-groom, was never to be trusted near horses.

Swaggering into the stables, Tolson found the owner talking to a couple of other men.

"Is this the stable needin' a first rate groom?" he called as he looked at one of the empty stalls.

The three gentlemen swung round. Tolson found himself facing a stranger as well as Louisa's father and husband.

"Get out!" yelled Mr George. "This is the villain I was telling you about. He can never be trusted near horses." As he spoke, he advanced on Tolson with his whip raised. "How dare you come here."

He brought the whip down, catching Tolson on the face. As one man ran the other bellowed: "You and that slut of a wife had best keep away from me or I'll put the police on you both."

My husband rushed back to the rooming house. He grabbed my purse, emptied it and took the few coins that it held then he grabbed me, shook me and screamed abuse because, according to him, I was the one Mr George really hated. He lifted his fist and crashed with all his force into my jaw. He shook me again, threw me on the floor, kicked me and, as he stormed out, screamed: "Get out. I never wanna see ya' again! Be here when I get back … you'll get worse.".

As I lay bleeding on the floor I worked out that I had been married for less than two years. Marriage had destroyed my life.

City Dirt – Foggy Skies

What for the next patch? It is shaped like a bell because London was full of ringing bells and it is the colour of grey skies and filthy streets.

What was I to do? I lay flat on my face on a dirty wooden floor with a bleeding broken tooth. I hurt everywhere. My husband's last words echoed in my head: "Be here when I come back and you'll get worse."

For a moment after the door slammed I had peace – I was alone, but I must get away. I pulled myself to my feet, lay Lucy's quilt on the bed, put my clothes and other bits onto it then tied it all into a bundle. For money I had just a few pence tucked into the hem of my skirt. I stumbled down the stairs but as I reached the front door the landlady appeared, took a quick look at my face and said:

"I heard most of that – bet the police'll be after him."

She grabbed my arm and pulled me into a different room. It was her part of the house and much cleaner than the rest! Her name was Jenny.

Jenny bathed my face and suggested that I let her pull the tooth. It was only staying in by a whisker so I nodded and she did it straight away. The pain was nothing when added to the rest of my miseries. She plugged the hole, gave me a tot of something foul and let me sleep.

Jenny looked after me for a few days. Her man asked around and found out the full story about my husband's meeting with Mr George. Tolson left London the same day, going north to his family. The police were definitely after him for the horse he had injured at Epsom. I was sure I'd seen the last of him.

I needed a job. Jenny told me that Mr William Stephen Dew, a hosier, was looking for a live-in housemaid so I decided to try for it. It would give me a roof over my head, food and a bit of money so Jenny told me where it was. The shop on Cheapside was found easily. There was a card in the window offering the job so I went in and saw two men behind the counter in a shop full of stockings and gloves of all colours and sizes.

"Are you looking for something special, ma'am?" smirked the tall skinny one.

"No, sir. I be interested in the job as housemaid."

Just then a customer came in so the skinny one waved me through to a pokey little room behind the shop. He sat down and scowled at me.

"Why do you think you could do this job?"

"I've been a housemaid since I was ten year old," I told him. "Started in the kitchen and by the time I was about fifteen I was upstairs maid and then a lady's maid."

"Why should I believe that?"

I gave him my references. He scarcely looked at them but he noticed the word "needlework".

"Can you do fine needlework?"

"Surely I can, sir."

"Prove it."

"Nothing with me now. I could show you something tomorrow."

"You're Irish so you're probably lying … If you're not, come back tomorrow with an example. What's happened to your mouth?"

"My husband beat me, broke my tooth and threw me out. I don't want to see him again."

"Where's your husband now?"

"Don't know. Left me and I heard he went north. He caused the death of a horse at Epsom. The police are after him"

"You bring that husband near here and I'll put the police on both of you. Be back tomorrow and bring some needlework."

When I went back the brothers looked at the patch-work quilt I'd made for Lucy then they showed me a pair of gloves where the stitching had come undone. I had to sit there and mend it while they watched. It was easy. Louisa's gloves had always needed mending so I knew how to do a good job. They muttered to each other before Mr William (the thin one) said they'd take me on for a four week trial. They'd expect me to keep the house and shop clean, serve their meals and mend any damaged goods. I was told the attic would be my room. I'd be paid and have a full Sunday off at the end of the trial.

"Be back to start work here at eight o'clock tomorrow. Always remember that every night we lock the door at nine o'clock when the curfew rings. Be out later and you'll never get into this house again." With that odd threat ringing in my ears, I left.

Jenny was pleased for me. She promised never to tell Tolson where I was and invited me to visit her on my days off. I asked her about the nine o'clock curfew.

"Oh that …"; she laughed. "Someone told me they've been ringing the curfew for about five hundred years."

"Is that a bit of craic?"

"What d'ya mean craic?"

"Fun ... nonsense."

"No, it's true. Started when London was much smaller. In those days you could hear the bell all over the city so it was rung at night to signal the end of the working day for apprentices."

"Five hundred years and they still do it? Sounds like blarney to me!"

"Well that's the story. London has lots of old, odd rules with stories to explain them."

The next day I was at that shop early. Mr Jake (the short one) opened the door and followed me upstairs to the attic, patting my behind whenever he could reach it! Oh lord, I thought, one of those who can't keep his hands to himself. All the way up he chirped:

"You'll like this job, you'll like this job. We'll get on well."

I didn't feel too chirpy when I noticed that there was no bolt on the door of my tiny room but I needn't have worried. That was the only time either of them ever came near the attic.

I left my bundle on the bed then went down to the kitchen, a dull, grubby space with a greasy window looking onto the area. There I met a grubby, greasy dame who cooked their breakfast and prepared soup or whatever they wanted for the midday meal. I would be expected to heat and serve it. She showed me where everything was. The rules were breakfast at nine o'clock and midday meal at two. Evenings the gents got their own, which meant that they usually went to a public house. It also meant that I had to get my own evening food so I started keeping bread and cheese in my room.

I served my first breakfast on time then Bet, the cook, left. I was on my own with the Dew brothers.

The job was fair. The house was small but not crowded with furniture so it was easy to sweep and dust. The shop was another matter. I don't think they'd tidied it for years. The first time I tackled it I found very dusty gloves and stockings on the floor behind boxes. They'd been there a long time. The Dews were surprised when I showed them what I'd found and even thanked me. I guessed that there may be more to find but I left that for another day.

The kitchen was horrible. I kept quiet for a few days then asked Bet if she would mind if I cleaned the window and got a bit more light into the place.

"Please yer'self. Yer must be getting' more pay 'n me to bother with winders."

I still didn't know what I was to be paid so I fixed the window but went slow on removing the rest of the grease.

The evening before my trial period was up, the gents invited me into the dining room. There was a box of stockings and gloves on the table that needed some mending, as well as matching threads and a packet of needles. Mr William spoke first.

"Have you heard from your husband?"

"No, sir."

"Be warned that if he causes any trouble you won't have this job long." He glared at me. "Now, Catharine, we are satisfied with your work but we need you to do repairs for the shop and to take over from Bet. As a maid of all work you will be paid eight pounds a year starting from tomorrow. You will be paid at the end of each quarter and you will have every second Sunday free. For the four weeks trial you did no sewing or cooking so we will pay you ten shillings only, with a little extra so that you can buy yourself a proper maid's dress and cap."

He put the ten shillings plus two extra on the table and looked directly at me for the first time. I didn't know what to say. I had no idea what my wage might be though it was less than I had earnt at the Manor. That pile of shillings was like a magnet. Mr Jake was bouncing around in his chair.

"You'll be happy here," he chirped, "and when you sew you can work in the dining room where there is a good light."

"When we are out, of course," was his brother's swift comment. "Well?" he barked.

"Thank you, sir," I said. "When does Bet finish?"

"She's finished. Prepare breakfast tomorrow before you go off for the day and make sure you're back in your room before we lock the door when the curfew bell sounds at nine o'clock."

That was it. I was hired and they cleared off to find their supper, while I scooped up my pay and counted it over and over.

Next day I visited Jenny and paid her for her care after Tolson's beating. It wasn't the first time she had met him. Tolson had stayed in her lodgings several times. She knew he was a drunkard and a liar but she was surprised to see me.

"Why?"

"Dunno. Didn't think he was interested in women. Saw him the day he'd been horsewhipped just before he beat you. Could see he was in a fury so I listened."

I told Jenny the story of my marriage. She didn't ask questions but she said I should keep off the streets as much as possible. Tolson could show up at any time.

I told Jenny about the deal I had struck with Mr Dew. She warned me to be careful.

"He's paying you rock-bottom for a maid of all work but you've agreed and you need the work and the shelter. At the end of your first year you'll be able to ask for an increase. See me before you do and I'll tell you what to say. Be careful how you use the money in your pocket – it has to last you for three months. Make sure you go to the secondhand shop in Newgate for that dress."

For the rest of my free day I wandered around the streets and lanes near Cheapside. I wanted to get to know where I was living. I saw barrow stalls where I could buy a penny loaf and a cup of milk or coffee and sometimes a hot potato. I worked out that if I went down Bow Lane by the church where the curfew was rung, I would probably get to the river. That would be for my next free Sunday.

The bell that rang the curfew was in a church called St Mary-le-Bow. It was such an odd name that I have always remembered it. The church had a high tower and spire so it was a useful landmark to guide me back to the shop when I went wandering.

Not far away was a whopping great church called St Paul's. I crept inside one day to have a look but I scuttled out quickly. A service was on and a very stern man near the front door looked down his nose at me and said "Sshush." It was too grand for me. Too big to see one end from the other. I never went in again.

For a year I put up with the conditions of my life. Slowly I got to know some of the servants in nearby houses and I explored London. Mr William started to use me to run messages and that way I found out where the shops were, where the toffs lived and how easy it was to get around once you knew the main streets and the river. I usually managed to make my wages last each quarter and I found that I could always borrow a few shillings, if I was really short, from that useful secondhand shop in Newgate. I didn't do that too often though. I'd never had money in my pocket so I was used to doing with very little.

On my free days I often found a comfy seat and watched the children. There were plenty of them. They didn't seem to go to Sunday School too often and they had lots of games that I enjoyed watching.

One was a skipping game played in a long line. As they skipped they sang *"Gay go up and gay go down to ring the bells of London town."* They'd go around the street as if they were following a special route. There were lots of verses. The first one was *"Oranges and lemons say the bells of Saint Clements"*. I had trouble understanding the rest but I knew that one of them was about "the great bell at Bow." I wondered what the game was really about.

The worst part of the job was the brothers Dew. I could never decide which of them was the older. Mr William was snarky and sneaky. When I was cleaning the shop he never took his eyes off me. I still found lost stockings from time to time. By the look on his face I suspected he had lost them on purpose to check if I was doing a proper job. His brother was strange.

Yes, Mr Jake was odd. He was a touchy person – he liked to touch things and people. In the shop I have seen him stand by a customer and stroke a fur collar. I have seen him stroke a child's hair or clothing. He would pick up a pair of satin evening gloves and just stand and run his finger and thumb up and down their length. When this happened he looked asleep. He was always patting me, usually on the bum, but if I left my mob cap off he'd stroke my hair. He was very gentle but if Mr William saw him he'd bark at him and send him off on an errand.

Occasionally Mr Jake would be up early and talk to me as I prepared breakfast. He never asked questions, he'd just tell me rambling tales about being a boy in London.

One day I asked him about the skipping game the children played – the little song that started *Gay go up and gay go down, to ring the bells of London Town*. He was delighted by the question and told me how all the bells in the area had their own song and they were listed in the rhyme the children sang. He told me that the line about the great bell that rang the curfew was *I do not know, said the great bell at Bow*. He told me too that the idea of ringing the curfew to get people off the streets was five hundred years old. He said that if I went down Newgate I could hear the bell at the Court say *When will you pay me?* He told me about other bells too, but the only other one I remembered was the first in the song: *Oranges and lemons say the bells of Saint Clements*. He was so pleased I was interested that he went around the house for days singing bits of the rhyme, until Mr William yelled at him.

In the end I decided he wasn't quite right in the head. When I asked Jenny about him she laughed. "Yes, I've heard about him. Oh he's a daftie no doubt but he's a nice one and harmless."

He was good in the shop with the customers because he really knew where to look for any article wanted. Mr William was impatient and would try to sell the first thing he found, but Mr Jake would ask gentle questions then go to exactly the right drawer or box and find what was needed. The two of them got on fairly well but Mr Jake was a better salesman while his brother looked after the money.

When my four quarters were nearly up I got ready to ask for a wage increase. By then I knew that other servants in the area were being paid ten guineas a year and most had every Sunday free. None of the others was doing needlework. I decided not to ask for more free time (I was still a bit nervous about Tolson) but to make it clear that I wanted those two extra guineas.

When the day came there was a row. While Mr Jake was out, Mr William called me into his office. He told me that although I gave reasonable service I was not worth any more money but I could have every Sunday off. I was so surprised I just stood and stared.

"Well?" he barked.

"Mr William, I don't want more free time."

"Why not?"

"No friends in London. Go to church sometimes. Nothing else."

"Something odd about that. Who you hiding from? Your husband turned up?"

This made me cranky. "I'm not hiding, sir, but I'm underpaid."

"What?" he yelled. "How dare you!"

I thought of Mrs O'Reilly and stood very straight. "Sir, I know three others who do the same housework but no needlework. All are paid ten guineas. One expects to go up to twelve guineas soon. I'm older than all of 'em. I've had more service experience … I'm asking for a rise."

He looked so furious that I thought he might strike me but just then Mr Jake came back.

"Have you told Catharine how pleased we are with her work?"

he chirped. While Mr William went purple in the face, Mr Jake turned to me and said:

"Your needlework is excellent. Since you've been here we haven't thrown away one pair of gloves or stockings damaged in the factory. We're planning a rise for you and extra free time. Ten guineas in future and every Sunday free."

At that I burst into tears.

"Don't cry," he chirped. "Come. Mr William let the lass sit down. She's so excited by your decision."

"Thank you, Mr Jake," I stammered. "Thank you, Mr William." I didn't dare look at him. I took off and ran upstairs to my own room.

How lucky that Mr Jake arrived when he did. Mr William was always the one to pay me and if I hadn't complained, he would have got away with not giving me a rise. Mr Jake would never have known. I felt I'd made an enemy in the household. I'd have to be careful in future.

My luck didn't last long. A few weeks later I was taking a Sunday stroll along the river when I was grabbed from behind.

"Well, stupid wife, what ya' up to?" It was Tolson. He didn't look in good shape. The whip cut across his face had left a deep scar and his clothes were old and grubby. He dragged me to a bench. Of course he'd found out about my job, in fact he'd been watching the shop for quite a while. He was nervous and jumpy because the police were still after him. He'd been north and then back to Ireland but was in trouble in both places.

"I want some money," he said. "I know where ya' work. I bet ya' earn a pretty penny from them old geezers. I want my share. Give it me or I'll come to that shop and tell 'em what a sneak-thief you are."

Mr William would love that and I'd lose my job.

"I have no money now," I tried.

"Don't believe you." He grabbed my reticule and turned it inside out. I had a shilling in it because I had planned to take Jenny out for tea. That plan went by the way. Tolson grabbed the money and as he raced off yelled: "I'll tell 'em you're a liar too."

I was in trouble. I had to keep Tolson away from the Dew brothers and I had to keep my hard-earned cash away from him.

I began to make mistakes in the kitchen. Twice, I burned the midday soup and I dropped a new loaf of bread into a pail of dirty water. Mr William swore at me and said he'd take the cost out of my next wages. Even Mr Jake was upset and stopped chatting to me.

Tolson made my life hell. He took to lurking near the shop watching for me to be sent out on a delivery, and I often was. He'd follow me and demand any tip I was given. He did well. I was known and liked and the tips were often generous. He, of course, went straight to the pub with the money.

He showed up on quarter day demanding a share of my wage. I refused but the result was a bruised arm and throat. I gave him half of my wage as well as all my tips.

I was too scared to go to the Police – he was my husband. I wasn't game to tell my bosses. They'd warned me about that. I was more frightened than I'd ever been in my life. I began to suffer from headaches and often couldn't eat my meals. Tolson's demands grew.

Just before Christmas, I found a pile of very dusty stockings hidden behind an old chest. No-one was in the shop so I scooped up the lot, put part of the pile on Mr William's desk and left the rest in my pocket. I planned to take them to that pawn shop in Newgate. I was known there as I'd both bought things and sometimes, near the end of the quarter, pawned the lovely patch-work quilt I'd made for Lucy. I always got it back when I had my wage.

I knew that selling Dew's stockings was risky but if it was successful, I might be able to buy Tolson off. At the worst I might lose my job but I was confident that I'd find another.

I knew that Mr William had started watching me very closely. He noticed a bruise on my arm and asked the cause. I said I didn't know.

He asked me if my husband had turned up. I said that I had seen him but had nothing to do with him. He warned me again that if there was any trouble he would sack me. I knew then that I might just as well give up the job next quarter day and disappear. I had eight pairs of stockings that were ready for sale. Next day, I pawned six pairs.

Before long I was dismissed. I was so scared of Tolson that I could think about little else. Mr William told me several times to clean out all the kitchen cupboards then accused me of laziness because it wasn't done. He went through the china and cutlery counting what was there. He found that several plates were cracked or chipped and he swore that there should have been four cups and saucers not just two. It didn't matter what I said. Mr Jake listened but didn't say a word. The next morning I dropped the frying pan, spreading their breakfast over the stone floor.

"I'm not well," I said and burst into tears.

"You'd better leave," they both said.

Mr William put a few shillings on the table and told me that the rest of my pay would make up for what I'd damaged. He told me to be out of the house within the hour.

What followed was a nightmare.

It was pouring with rain and Tolson was lurking in the street. He saw I was weeping.

"Why ya' got ya' clothes bundle?"

"Sacked."

He grabbed my arm and slapped my face hard.

"I knew you was a stupid slut. Lost a job that was a good little earner." He slapped me again. "What ya gunna do now? If yer think Jenny'll help, yer wrong. I've warned her about you."

I staggered down the street to the door of St Mary-le-Bow. It was open so I went in. I didn't think Tolson would follow and I was right.

"I know where t'find yer when I want to," he yelled.

I crept into the shadows and down the stairs towards the crypt. It was dark and horrible but it was dry. I stopped, sat on the steps and tried to think what to do next. I had the few shillings Mr Dew had given me and two pairs of stockings. I waited till it was nearly dark and went out and bought a bit of food then back into the church before the door was locked.

I hid there for two nights until the Verger found me. He was a nice old man but he wouldn't let me stay. I moved from place to place but I ended up at the pawn shop, got rid of the last two pair of stockings and, as I left, ran straight into Tolson. He took my coins and disappeared.

I was lost. I stumbled back to the church but the Verger was standing in the doorway and he waved me off. It was raining still so I crept along the wall but shelter didn't last long. Bow Lane led to the Thames and I let it take me all the way down to the wharf. I walked to the edge of the timbers and looked at the river. Despite the rain the tide was out and all I saw was mud. My momentary thought of drowning myself was forgotten. The mud stank!

I moved back into the shelter of some buildings, found a doorway that wasn't hiding someone else and curled up in a ball, felt my pocket to make sure that Lizzie's button was safe and with it in my hand finally slept.

I existed that way for a few more days. There was so little daylight that it was best to find a dry spot and stay there as long as possible, knowing that if I moved I'd lose it to some other lost soul like me. A big city is a cruel place to be in when you have no home.

At last the rain stopped and the sun appeared. It made such a difference that I forgot to slink from shadow to shadow and instead marched up the hill away from the stinking river. I didn't get far. A hand fell on my shoulder and Mr William Dew told a constable that I was the thief he wanted arrested. It was almost a relief.

When will you pay me, said the bells at Old Bailey. They rang for me then. I knew I would have to pay but I didn't know how.

Wonderful Colourful Sea

I shall have fun with this patch. I shall create the sea.

I was tried at the Old Bailey and of course I was found guilty. Mrs O'Reilly, you would have been ashamed of me. I tried to stand up for myself as you liked me to but it didn't work at the Old Bailey.

Mr William Dew spoke first. He said he was there when I was taken into custody and that I had a ticket from the shop to show that I had pawned his stockings. He said he knew the make of the stockings and that he had missed 'ten dozen of them.' That made me furious. If Dew had lost ten dozen, it wasn't me that took 'em.

The two witnesses against me were young fellows who worked at the pawn shop. The first said he knew me. He made quite a long speech:

"I am shopman to Mr Flemming of Newgate Street. This six

pairs of stockings were pawned at our shop on 26 January. I took them in and gave the duplicate – it was a woman but I do not know whether a young woman or an old one."

When I heard that I spoke up: "Do not you know me by buying new articles at your shop?"

"She has bought articles but I do not know whether she pawned these."

The constable was asked to give his evidence and he said that he had searched my purse when I was taken into custody and that Mr Dew had found pawn duplicates in my purse.

The other shopman gave evidence that the stockings had been pawned by an old woman.

I was cross about this 'old woman' stuff, but of course I had worn a heavy veil on both days that I pawned those stockings. I thought I must make another effort to get some sympathy.

"I was unfortunate in my marriage," I said. "My husband deserted me ... I had a little bag in which I kept some duplicates. I took them out of the bag and this duplicate of my master's property came out first. It had been put in by someone unknown by me."

Nobody listened. I was quickly found guilty and sentenced. My payment was transportation to Sydney for seven years. A high price for eight pairs of stockings worth four shillings and three-pence.

Six weeks in the loathsome London prison taught me many things. The women were a mixed bunch. A few pretended to be holy, sang hymns all the time and tried to get us to say our prayers at night. They soon gave up. Others were very rough. Most were somewhere in between and that's where I fitted. I shared a prison cell with a few of each sort and learnt some names and stories.

There was a murderer waiting to be hanged, several pick-pockets, a poisoner who might also be hanged, two or three prostitutes and a few thieves, like me, a title I now had thanks to Tolson.

While we were in the prison a very proper lady visited more than once. She said we should aim to improve our lives in the new land. She gave each of us a package of materials and sewing threads and needles. She had two packages for me, and as she gave them to me she whispered: "Louisa sent one." I was amazed.

I unpacked it carefully and found enough fabric for a new dress and matching bonnet with a collection of small pieces of cloth for a patchwork quilt. There were four pairs of drawers – they weren't new but they were the sort Louisa always wore. There were also two aprons like Mrs O'Reilly's. In the pocket of one was a note written by that good woman: "T told G who made sure L knew. God bless and keep you, Catharine."

It made me weep to realise that I wasn't forgotten.

That note answered a puzzle I had. When I was arrested Mr William Dew was with the Constable. I wondered how I had been found out. I guessed that someone had snitched. Tolson shadowed me to the shop the first time I pawned those stocking and, of course, he took the money then and on the last time I ever went there.

If my dear husband told Dew that I had been pawning stockings he would have earned a tip. Tolson would do anything for a shilling.

Although I hated Tolson, I realised that he had, in the end, done me one favour. He made sure George heard the story which meant Louisa heard it too. The package I received from Louisa gave me something to do during the voyage, and it helped me hold up my head and tell my companions about my kind friends. When the world has thrown you to the bottom of the heap, it's very important to believe in yourself and stand tall. Louisa's gift made that possible.

The day I was taken to the ship I watched two guards write about me in a big book. They left the Jane out of my name. If they couldn't get that right how much more was wrong? They said I was twenty four, which was as good as I could guess and that I was married and could read and write. Correct. They said I was a cook, housemaid and needlewoman. Correct. They measured me and said I was four feet, ten and a half inches. Don't know about feet and inches but I do know that I was shorter than nearly everyone else I had ever met. They noticed that my hair and eyes were brown, but they forgot the curls and they said I had a ruddy and freckled face and yes, they mentioned the tooth I had lost and the scar near my thumb.

How did I get that scar? I think it goes back to when I was working in the fields with my Da. I was using a stick to dig out small weeds and ran the pointy end into my hand. Something like that, anyway.

As we were marched through the streets of London to the docks, all the church bells seemed to shriek at us. Then we were on the ship *Mary* and off to New South Wales. Less than three months passed between my crime and my banishment, but it felt more like three years.

The next part of my life had begun. London was left behind, replaced by a ship that relied on the water beneath it and the wind in its sails to move anywhere. I came to love it.

The sea can be grey with slow heaving waves. The sea can be sparkling and gentle. The sea can throw up green waves much taller than the ship. The sea can suddenly stop moving in the middle of the wide blue ocean where there is nothing to see. The sea can be frightening. The sea is amazing.

I was a good sailor – I was never seasick once. Most of the women were seasick sometimes and some never stopped heaving till we got to Sydney and the ship stopped heaving! Fancy being sick for nearly five months! That's how long it took us to get from the Thames River to Port Jackson.

At first we had to stay in our quarters in the belly of the ship but the covers were kept open when it wasn't raining or the seas weren't high, and gradually, as the sailors got to know us, we were allowed to spend time on deck. Long days sitting dreaming in the sun gave me time to think back over my mistakes in London and to imagine what might come next.

Of all the women on the *Mary* there was only about a dozen of us who really liked to sew. The sailors expected us to mend their clothes and as we had to do their laundry it made sense to mend the stuff while it was clean. Everyone had turns at the laundry but Harriet and Maria and I did most of the mending. We guessed that if we helped the sailors they might help us, and they did. All prisoners were let out on deck most days and a sailor found a spot where the three of us could sit out of the wind. That was a great bonus, since on windy days the only other place we could go was in the hold and that place stank of dirty bodies, unwashed beds and latrine buckets.

Once on deck I began to watch how a ship worked. I soon realised that one or two of the sailors were cruel and enjoyed making life bad for the young members of the crew. Harriet, who was very proper, watched too. It was she who taught me the word 'sadistic' the day the youngest was whipped then sent straight up the rigging to the top of the mast. The young fellow was the Captain's cabin boy. Early that day he'd dropped the Captain's hat which annoyed the bo'sun. The boy was tied to the mast with the sun full on him then whipped till his shirt was in ribbons and his back ripped and bleeding. Afterwards they threw a bucket of sea water over him then sent him up the rigging, with two sailors behind him with orders to whip his legs if he slowed down.

It was terrible to watch. The more the boy stumbled the more his tormentor laughed. Even the boys behind the victim didn't want to whip him again, but occasionally had to prod him because they knew they could be the next for the cat o' nine tails. The cabin boy began to sway badly. I thought he might fall but just at that point the Captain appeared and the terrible business stopped. The boy wasn't seen on deck again for weeks. Harriet called the bo'sun a sadistic bully. Always after, when I thought about Tolson, that is the label I put on him.

I liked Harriet but she wasn't a close friend. She was very secretive. She wouldn't tell anything about her life or why she'd been transported. If you asked she just said: "That is past and doesn't matter anymore."

Maria White was a different sort of person. She liked a laugh and a joke and she had no hesitation in telling me that she robbed her master. I think she was proud that she'd got the better of a man in a fight over money.

She liked to sing too and with her leading us we all learnt the ship's favourite: "What shall we do with the drunken sailor …" She also taught me a gentle little song called Strawberry Fair and I taught her Molly Malone.

Hoping to find out whatever we could about New South Wales, we got chatty with one or two of the sailors. One old fellow was quite knowledgeable and told us about Sydney Town and the rocky island near Sydney Cove called Cockatoo Island. Its name came from the white birds with yellow crests that lived on it. He also said that one of the natives told him that they called the island Waremah (or something like that). We asked him what the natives were like. He said that some were very friendly but that others were too fond of rum. He didn't seem to know a lot about them.

He also told us about the Female Factory at Paramatta. He was sure that all of us would go there.

Because of the name, I hated the place before I saw it. I hadn't worked at a Hosiers' shop without learning what a Glove Factory or a Stocking Factory was. A Factory was a great, dark barn of a place where people toiled at nasty, dangerous machines to turn raw materials into saleable goods. I wasn't going to work a nasty machine. I wasn't raw material for anyone to change. Worse still, for two years I'd mended damaged goods that came out of factories, so I feared that this place could damage us. No matter what I said, some of the sillier women on the ship thought it must be some sort of holiday house. Even Harriet didn't seem to understand that we were being treated like saleable goods. I made up my mind that I wasn't something to be re-made and passed on.

Of course there were women on the ship who were happy to sell themselves to anyone. Most of the sailors knew this and there were times when you stayed on deck, rather than come face to face with a bit of very rough trade. Ugh! It wasn't my idea of pleasure. Just imagine how awful if you found that a child was coming! I hated what had happened to me but I decided that since it had, I must get on and do my best to make something of myself in this new country. From now on, anything that happened would be up to me. Somehow I would keep Mrs O'Reilly as my model and try to be dignified and in control of my own life. I would think tall and strong.

At last the journey came to an end. For several days we sailed along the coast and could see yellow sandy beaches and little bays and rocky fingers pointing out at the sea. At last we changed direction. The bow was pointed straight at a gap between two mighty, rocky cliffs. We sailed through a rough stretch of water between The Heads, the sea calmed and we were in Port Jackson.

Colours of a New Land

This patch will have two pictures on a piece of pale fabric. On top, my first view of the colony on 7 September 1835. I'll embroider Sydney Cove with little boats on the water and dark green trees fencing the whole place. Underneath will be my first view of the Female Factory, a harsh and colourless building.

Sydney didn't impress me too much and Cockatoo Island scared me. It was all rock and covered by big, screaming white birds. Some flew to the ship and settled in the rigging. They were very big with cruel hooked beaks. They screamed whenever they flew and when they settled, they raised the crest on their head so that sulphur coloured feathers could be seen.

When I looked at this new town there were so few people to see that my eye went immediately to its surroundings. It was perched on the edge of a small cove that was part of an enormous bay. To the right was a great rocky hill and to the left a bit of flattish land. Behind it and everywhere I looked were trees that were packed together and looked dark green or grey. I worked out that their colour depended a lot on whether or not the sun was shining on them. There was a distinct smell in the air. The sailors said it was eucalyptus, a name that was new to all of us but we soon learnt the word and the smell. It was to be the backdrop to the rest of our lives. Trees here are mostly eucalypts but we all call them gum trees.

I didn't set foot in Sydney Town for years. Instead, most of us were herded into small boats and taken straight up river to the Female Factory. It took more than a day, so overnight the boats anchored and we dossed down on the river bank on the bedding we had brought from the *"Mary"*. The night was cool and so full of rustles and squeaks and croaks and grass whispering that, on the whole, I thought it was more interesting than London's bells. It reminded me of the farm noises I used to hear when I was living in that shed with Da. It didn't frighten me at all.

When we arrived at Parramatta all my fears proved right. The stone building mostly had two floors, the bottom was cells and the top was the factory. There were machines and roughly spun flax that we were expected to weave into the ugly, stiff cloth used for men's working clothes. No one in charge seemed to know how to mend the looms or how to teach newcomers to use the machines. There was real overcrowding in the cells, so many of us had to sleep upstairs on the floor near the machines. I was glad I still had the mouldy mattress from the ship. At least I knew I was the only person who had slept on it.

In time Maria worked out how to use the loom so she wove cloth, then I was shown how to cut it and sew it into the loose trousers and jackets that convict men wore. It was the first time I had ever really seen how cloth could be shaped into clothing and, though I hate to admit that anything good came out of the factory, this was to be useful knowledge.

The Factory was disgusting but also a bit odd. Overcrowding was bad because, as well as prisoners, the place was a home for old women who couldn't work anymore. Usually they were ex-convicts who nobody wanted. It was also a sort of laying-in place for younger women who were expecting babies. Some were still convicts who had been assigned or even married to a free man but were not wanted when a baby was on the way. When we arrived more than half of the people in that place were not prisoners. Because of the overcrowding we were able to wander in and out more or less as we wished, as long as we did a bit of work and were there for roll call.

Harriet had disappeared. She didn't come up-river with us. We never saw her again. She must have been assigned as a servant to someone who lived at Port Jackson – someone who knew she was arriving on our ship.

Maria was still with me and we teamed up to make the best of a bad job. We decided to try to get assigned to work for a free settler. We soon found out that, because of the classification we'd been given, we were unlikely to be assigned to anyone. We had both robbed our Masters so we were not in the top classification. We were stuck in Parramatta.

Another odd thing about the place was that day by day we'd find new women had arrived and others had disappeared. The new ones might be off a new ship, but more likely they had been in trouble with the police and were serving time for something done at the colony. Some were really pleasant people who had been assigned to a free settler as servants, then were found not suitable and sent back to the Factory. Half the time they didn't know what they'd done wrong. One said the man in charge wanted a prostitute for the convicts he was employing. She objected so she was sent back. One master didn't like the food the new servant cooked, so back she went. Another woman had a very bad cough so she came back too. These stories made me a bit suspicious about the assignment system so I wasn't worried that I couldn't use it.

The constant coming and going of these different women confused the staff. That was a fact that people like us, who learnt the system quickly, could use. We went walkabout (my first new word since I came to the colony) and were never missed so used the time to learn our way around Parramatta.

The other odd thing about the place was that it was a marriage market! Yes we were seen as saleable goods. Women could let the Superintendent know that they were willing to marry, then if a man arrived at the gate looking for a wife he'd be introduced to the willing women and make his choice. I soon found out that I would have no show in that game because the first question asked was "Are you married?" Well of course I was. Tolson hung round my neck. There was nothing I could do but wait for some other way of getting out of the place.

As the weather became hotter, Maria and I got into the habit of leaving the factory after the evening meal and going for a walk along the river bank. It was cooler out there and we'd meet other women. Quite often men would be hanging around too. Some were looking for a wife but most were just looking for a woman for the night. Maria and I kept our distance unless we liked someone and we did find a few blokes, ex-convicts, who were reasonably behaved. One was a funny Irish fellow called Phelan. He and I would put on our worst Irish accents and tell tall tales about our home country, though I don't think either of us wanted to go back there. Still, we kept our friends laughing which was good.

We eventually taught them all to sing *Molly Malone* and our rowdy chorus was often loud enough to annoy anyone who heard it. We had fun and changed the words to suit where we were:

In Sydney's new city, where convicts are pretty,
we first set our eyes on sweet Molly Malone,
as she wheeled her wheel barrer,
through lanes rough and narrer,
yelling won't work for your sir until I am free.

Maria became quite fond of Phelan. She thought he was a bit of a dope (which he was) but he was good natured and strong. He was an ex-convict who worked anywhere he could and always visited us if he was in Parramatta. She began to think that she should try and marry him, because she was sure she could stand over him and get him working regularly. In this place people willing to work hard did well.

At last the horrible year 1835 came to an end. There was a lot of carry-on at the Factory and we were all given a small tot of rum with our evening meal. We were then told that we were free until roll call on the first day of 1836.

Naturally Maria and I went out. I was wearing, for the first time, the dress I made from the material Louisa had sent me. It was a very pretty cotton which suited the humid weather we were experiencing. I felt very special. Phelan was waiting for us with a couple of his mates and we all wandered off together. Phelan had a bottle of grog which, he said, was better than rum but when I smelt it I told him I didn't want my share. It reminded me of rotten eggs. Well they all got merry on it and Maria and Phelan wandered off together.

I stayed for a while thinking they'd be back soon but they didn't reappear. The other two fellows were drunk and asleep so I set off for the Factory by myself. I was nearly there when I met two men I'd never seen before. One was in uniform, the other in ordinary workman's clothing. They were very drunk. They spoke to me so I said "Happy New Year" and kept walking. I didn't get far.

"Ain't that Molly Malone?" one of them muttered.

"Yep," said the other. "Let's check out her cockles and mussels." Before I could do much I was dragged into the bushes, my mouth was blocked, my clothes ripped and they had a merry time. I had no chance of saving myself though I tried.

I staggered back to the Factory with a black eye, neither shoes nor stockings on my feet, my beautiful new dress ruined and my drawers and shift ripped and filthy. Even at his most brutal, Tolson hadn't hurt me as much as those two.

I curled up in a corner of the work room and wept. When Maria returned she was full of cheer because she had decided that she would marry Phelan. Seeing the state I was in, she calmed down and helped me clean myself. She persuaded me that I must report the matter to Rev Samuel Marsden, who was on the Board of Management of the Factory and was the Superintendent of Government Affairs in Parramatta. Next day I saw the matron and she took me to Marsden but I'm not sure that he believed my tale at first, although he was horrified when matron told him of the bruises on my body and the ruin of my clothes.

A few weeks later I guessed that I was in trouble. Out of that filthy event I would get a child. It seemed as if 1836 would be another bad year.

I had often wondered what being a mother would be like but I knew that a child born this way would carry a heavy load. Who was its father? Would it be healthy? How could I care for it in prison? Should I offer myself for marriage? Maria and I talked about it a lot. Maria told Phelan who was quite upset and said "She must get married. I'll have her." Maria wasn't pleased with that offer and nor was I. I didn't see how I could marry him or anyone. Tolson again!

I wasn't the first prisoner who found herself expecting a child after she arrived in the colony. Some were too friendly with sailors on the journey out, some got too friendly with ex-convicts and soldiers who hung around the Factory, and some were like me, forced. When the matron was told she always wanted to know the name of the man involved and I heard that the usual answer was a dirty chuckle followed by "Rev Marsden, Miss." Of course it was never true, it was just that he visited the Factory frequently. He was a hard man and had a lot of control over which prisoners got a chance to better themselves and which were left on the scrap heap. He was generally hated.

Oddly, I got on fairly well with him. I occasionally went to his church services and once he asked if any of us was willing to do some sewing for him. Nobody offered, but I was so fed up with having nothing interesting to do that the next time I saw him I offered to help.

The work wasn't hard and I earned eight pence for each piece I did. It gave me a chance to experiment with something I had learnt when I looked after Lucy. Her Mam was an expert and she had shown me what to do. It was called "drawn thread work". It was only possible if the fabric was a good linen. The weave and the weft had to be absolutely straight, so that you could draw out a thread and make a pattern.

Reverend Marsden wanted some simple white cloths of several different sizes made from material sent out from Ireland. Catharine the Irish prisoner worked on Irish linen for the English church in New South Wales. What a laugh! He knew about the baby coming and eventually I asked him if it might be possible for me to marry Phelan.

Normally he'd roar something nasty like

"You're a married, woman! What do you mean by daring to suggest that you ignore your vows and your promises to God and take on another husband?" For once, he didn't do that. He asked me about my marriage and where it had taken place.

"Dublin, sir."

" Ha! Dublin! I didn't know you were a Catholic."

"Don't think I am, sir."

"What do you mean? What church did you attend with your parents?"

"Never went to church, sir. Mam died and Da was away working. Sister Lizzie died and I never went to church till Miss Louisa took me to the English church."

He looked a bit surprised about this and asked me to say the Hail Mary and make the sign of the cross.

I told him I didn't know how to do the sign and that I had no idea what the Hail Mary was. Of course that wasn't true. Bridget taught me both years ago. I didn't want him to decide I was a Catholic so I fibbed.

"Where did your husband come from?"

"He said he was a Yorkshireman."

"Hmm. He could be a Catholic." He thought a bit then asked, "Where was the wedding held?"

I had trouble answering this question. "Well sir, I really don't know."

"What do you mean, woman? How do you know that you're married?"

"Well, sir, Tolson had a job to go to in England so when he persuaded me to marry him, he said he'd make all the arrangements. Two days later we walked to a small building in a part of Dublin I'd never visited. The Housekeeper came with me as my witness and the ceremony was over quite quickly. We signed some papers that the Reverend put in front of us and that was that. We walked my witness back to her home and next day we left for England."

"Did you keep your Marriage Certificate? … Did you have a wedding ring?"

"Well I saw the certificate that day but Tolson took it and put it in his pocket. I never saw it again. I had a ring but Tolson pawned it before he disappeared."

"Hmm," he muttered. "If he was from Yorkshire he was likely a Catholic and if it was all organised in such a short time, I don't believe that such a marriage would be legal. Who do you want to marry?"

"Phelan, sir. He has offered to look after me and the baby."

"Right. Bring him to see me tomorrow and I'll post the banns. I'll write to Sydney to get the marriage approved."

I rushed off to see Maria and she was pleased for me although she still had a fancy for Phelan. He was in town so she found him and he agreed to go with me the next day to see the Superintendent.

On 4 April 1836 the banns were posted at the church and I looked forward to getting out of the factory, but sometime during the three weeks that had to pass before the ceremony could be performed, news came from Sydney Town that the recommendation wasn't accepted. I was a married woman and could not marry again without proof of my husband's death. I knew I could never meet that rule. I was stuck as Catharine Tolson for the rest of my life and there would soon be another little person with that name.

Despite my plans and hopes, the Factory had thoroughly re-made me.

Phelan went off up bush to work and Maria and I did what we could to prepare for the new one. She told me that she intended to marry Phelan herself if he came back with decent earnings and she offered to take my baby as theirs, to get it out of the horrible Factory.

I said I'd think about the idea.

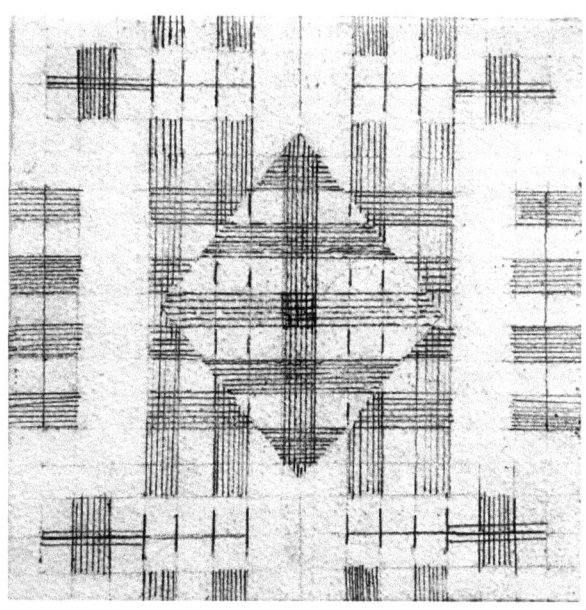

Drawn Thread Stitches

A new patch for a painful and sad but lovely time. I want to show my Jane that she is not forgotten even though she and I hardly got to know each other. Her patch will show all the drawn thread stitches I know.

My first child was born on 1 October 1836. The closer it came to the time of her birth the less well I felt. I was lodged with other women expecting a child and a mixed lot we were. Some were women who came to the Colony free, others were ex-convicts and the rest were like me, still prisoners. We convicts knew that we'd be able to keep our little ones with us, until they were four and were transferred to the nearby Orphan School. We'd be able to reclaim them when we left the Factory. This all sounded reasonable because I knew that I might be able to get a job at the School.

Maria was still talking about marrying Phelan and adopting my child but I never agreed to it. I wanted to find out what it was like to be a mother before I agreed to give the child away.

The first of October arrived and with it my daughter. She was very small but I am a small person too so I wasn't surprised. The matron and the midwife thought that she was too small and light but I couldn't see that. She was like a little me. I sang to her in my own way and didn't know where the words came from. Perhaps my Mam had sung it to me. The only word was 'macuosla'. I called her Jane, my other name. On the fourth day of December I took her to St John's Church at Parramatta and Reverend Marsden baptised her, wiping her with one of the cloths I had made for him.

Jane was not a bonny baby. She didn't eat well and I found that I didn't have a lot of milk for her. The matron did what she could for me but she didn't know a lot about sickly babies. They were rare at the Factory. Despite the drab and dirty surroundings, most of the babies born at the colony were strong. Little Jane was the exception. Maria loved her and thought that she'd have a better chance if she was away from that place. I still hadn't agreed but in the end none of that mattered.

One morning I woke up to find that my daughter had died. I rushed out to find Matron who didn't seem at all surprised.

"Maybe it's all for the best," she said. "She was very weak."

"No, no," I screamed. "You just didn't know how to help her. Nobody cared." I held the little body tight in my arms and wouldn't let matron take her. I wept and screamed till Maria came and sat with me.

"You must let her go, Catharine. She came into the world because of wickedness and it was too much for her little body to bear. You must let me take her to Matron so she can be buried."

I resisted for quite a while but I knew that Maria was right. I cut off part of the quilt I had made for little Lucy and wrapped my Jane in it. I kissed her once more before Maria took her and that was the last time I saw her.

There was a small burial plot behind the Factory where babies born dead were placed and Matron decided that Jane should go there. I never knew quite where she was but I was told that Reverend Marsden said a prayer for her. That didn't stop me cursing the men who had caused this and I started being rude to everyone in charge. It was a useless way to behave but I had to scream at someone.

Matron got tired of my tantrums and being called 'a fecking old harridan'. She hauled me into her office and told me to pull myself together.

"You're being foolish and you know it. You have a lot to offer so why behave like the lowest street girl?"

I glowered at her.

"You did everything you could have done for your child and I admire you for it. You knew how to look after her. Most new mother's don't."

"Course I did … had enough practice."

"What do you mean?"

I told her about Lizzie and Louisa and Lucy. She was surprised.

"You've had more nursing experience than anyone else here. What about doing some more?"

I shrugged.

"You know about the orphan school we have here, well it needs a nurse. It's a paid job. I'll give you a trial. You can report over there tomorrow."

I was astonished. I had been so rude to her. "Thankee Matron … I'm sorry I've been so stupid." I grabbed my brains and gave her a proper bob.

When I told Maria she was really pleased because she wanted to marry Phelan, but didn't like leaving me when I was so sad. I told her not to worry about me but to marry her man.

I enjoyed my job at the School Hospital, though it lasted less than a year. It began before Maria and Phelan married in April 1837. I attended their wedding and saw them leave the Factory arm in arm. I wasn't sure where they were going, neither were they, but I wished them well and gave Maria a bonnet I had made for her with her name embroidered on it. She seemed pleased. I hope they had a happy life. I never saw them again, though I heard once they'd gone to Tasmania. That could be true.

I was now without a real friend at the Factory. I stopped going out for evening walks and put a lot of effort into my new job. I also got to know an old lady who had been in the Factory longer than me. She hardly ever talked and she sat in a corner of the workroom, fiddling with balls of thread. One day I sat down next to her and asked her what she was doing.

"Lace."

"Show me."

Reluctantly she showed me what was in her lap. There were two big balls and when I looked I could see they were connected. One was plain thread and the other was a strip of lace.

"How do you turn thread into something different?"

She cackled and from her sleeve drew out a piece of polished wood with a hook at one end.

"Don't you ken crochet when t'is under your nose?" she said.

I didn't but I was immediately interested. "I want to learn. Will you teach me?"

She cackled again. "Tell Matron and ask her for a hook."

Matron took some persuading but she found me a hook and my lessons started. My teacher was Scottish. Her name was Heather and she was free to leave the Factory but she was too old to get a job, and was very nearly blind. None the less she could produce long strings of lace about half a thumb wide and Matron had a little business with ladies in Sydney who wanted it to trim their bonnets.

A lady would send a skein of wool or a large reel of thread to Matron who gave it to Heather. She was paid when the job was done. It earnt her just enough to help her buy extra food or clothing.

From my work at the Orphan School I earnt seven pounds a

year. I felt very rich, even though I didn't see the money for a few years. I enjoyed working with the children. I even taught them *"Oranges and lemons"* but it was a dirty place and I finally picked up an infection, so in March 1838 I had to leave the job. I was replaced immediately. I wasn't given time to recover. That made me cranky but it turned out to be a good thing.

One day Matron called me into her office. She had a guest, Mrs Wilshire. The lady had heard about my needlework from Reverend Marsden. By this time, the so-called assignment system had been abandoned and the only way out of the Factory was by serving your time, or by being properly employed by someone. Mrs Wilshire wanted to employ an experienced needlewoman. She lived out Liverpool way and I could tell by her dress and her speaking that she was truly a lady. I collected a few pieces of work to show her and she said that she would make her decision by the next day.

I knew she'd seen one or two other women so I was afraid I'd miss out. I didn't sleep at all that night. The next morning quite early, I was told that I had the job. I said goodbye to Heather, packed up my few bits and pieces, was given the money I had earned and when Mrs Wilshire arrived I was ready and waiting. I was, more or less, free. What a wonderful day!

The Wilshire's had a very nice home about twenty miles south of Parramatta. There was a cook, a housemaid and a gardener as well as me, and we all had rooms above the stable. We were all convicts. Cook and the gardener were a married couple so they had the biggest room. The housemaid and I had room each. For the first time in my life I had a room all my own with a bed, a clothes cupboard, a small toilet table with basin, jug and chamber pot (mismatched but real china), a comfortable chair and a table with a good lamp. It was wonderful. Apart from the tiny attic at the Dews, this was the first time in my life I'd been on my own, could keep my clothes tidy and read or sleep or dream without being disturbed by anyone.

Mr Wilshire was a big business man. I think he knew everyone important in the Colony. His wife was a very good mistress. She knew how things should be done in a gracious house and she had waited for nearly two years for the arrival of special materials she had ordered from England, so that she could provide proper linen for her home. There was a whole bolt of heavy cotton for sheets and pillowcases and another of Irish linen for the table. I had lots to do. There were five children in the family as well as guest rooms and all had to be provided with new bedding.

Mrs Wilshire, who I always called ma'am, wanted the beds done first so I had a lot of hemming to do. One day when I was dreaming, I ran the needle into my finger and bled all over the sheet I was holding. I was very upset but Mrs Wilshire wasn't cross. She showed me how to use cold water to remove bloodstains, put a small bandage on my finger, and back I went to the job.

Sometimes, Mrs Wilshire's young sister Sarah came to stay at the house. She was a lively lady about my age and we'd work together. We'd start at the same time to hem a sheet and see who finished first. It was a race, which made the job more interesting. While we worked she told me a lot about Sydney Town.

When hems were done I trimmed one end of the sheets and the frill on the pillowcases with lace that Mrs Wilshire had made. Attaching the lace needed special care so I usually did it in the evening in the quiet of my own room. Seeing the quality of Mrs Wilshire's crochet work, I knew mine wasn't very good at all so I asked her to help me. She did, but her main lesson was "Practise, Catharine. Practise."

It was the same lesson I heard from the farmer's wife when I was learning to sew.

It was exciting to be able to spend my pay as I pleased. I bought some material to make a new dress and Mrs Wilshire gave me Saturday afternoon free. What a joy. On Sunday no work was done in the household except by the cook. The whole Wilshire family went to church and sometimes I went too. It was a long walk but it was good to be in the fresh air.

When the bedding was all made we began on the table linen. There was a lot of special handwork to be done. In the corner of dinner cloths and napkins I used a pale ecru thread to embroider the letter W to a design that Mrs Wilshire gave me. It was very elegant. (Sarah taught me that word.) On afternoon tea linens I did a drawn-thread pattern. I really enjoyed my work. When Mrs Wilshire had ladies in for afternoon tea, I sometimes helped by serving the guests and it was exciting when any of them praised the linen. Mrs Wilshire always told them that I had done most of the hand work. That was generous. It sometimes led to requests for me to do work for one of the guests. Mrs Wilshire was very kind. She always encouraged me to accept such chances which increased my savings.

Mrs Wilshire also taught me a lot more about waiting at table. As a girl I had to wait on senior staff at the Manor, but now I learnt all the dos and don'ts needed for quality. It was to be very useful later on.

Mr Wilshire was a busy man but he didn't forget me. In September 1839 I received a Ticket of Leave, as long as I remained in Liverpool. I didn't want to leave there, I was in a very good position.

Mr Wilshire spent a lot of time in Sydney because of his Tannery at Brickfield Hill. It was such a big part of his business that I heard talk that he might move his home into Sydney. That's what happened. Mrs Wilshire told me of the plans and said that my Ticket would be changed to Sydney, so that I could stay in their employment. That suited me.

I still had about two years before I would be free, but once in Sydney I began to feel as if that day might really come. I was now a trusted servant and often went on messages for both Mr and Mrs Wilshire. They were fair people. It was fun to learn the growing town and to wonder what I might do when I was able to choose for myself. I didn't hope to be wealthy but I hoped to be respected. I believed that inside I was as good as anyone else. If I remembered all that I had learnt from Mrs O' Reilly, Louisa, Lucy's mother and Mrs Wilshire, I knew that I could be a good woman.

One day there was an important letter to deliver to Mr Wilshire so I was sent to Brickfield Hill to the Tannery. When I got there I wasn't sure where to go. It was a huge place with many different buildings and an unpleasant smell. I paused at the gate and looked around. A young fellow was coming out.
"Are you lost?"
"No. I'm going to Mr Wilshire's office."
"Ah ha! You're lost. If you weren't, you'd know where to go."
Here's a cocky one, I thought. Just what I can do without.
"I'll show you the way." He took off and I followed him past a series of buildings to a small one with a well painted door. "Here you are. Just ask in there." He pushed the door open for me and I went in. Once inside I saw a smart looking man sitting at a desk. He looked up.
"What do you want?" he asked.
"Just to hand this letter to Mr Wilshire." I opened my basket and showed it to him.
"Wait there." He disappeared through another door. Mr Wilshire appeared.
"Well Catharine, what have you got for me?" I did a bob and handed him the letter. "Ah yes, just what I was waiting for. Thank you for bringing it." He reached into his pocket and put a shilling in my hand. That was a surprise but I did another bob as I said "Thank you" then he went back into his office while I went out the door.
Who was just outside? Yes it was him, the chatty one.
"You're such a little thing, I thought you might need help to find

the gate. My name's Will Maber, what's yours?"

"I'm Catharine. I work for the Wilshire family. What do you do?"

"What's yer other name?"

"None of your business. Anyway what do you do?"

"I am a ladies shoe maker. I'm now a free man. I intend to make the best shoes and boots in Sydney. I'm going to have my own shop and I'll do business with Mr Wilshire because I'll buy my leather from him. I've been here this morning meeting one of the bosses to make arrangements for my business. I think that although I didn't want to come here, this new land will be good to me."

Here's a halfpenny wag, I thought. Really full of himself. Wonder what they sent him out here for? Talking the hind leg off a donkey, probably.

"Do you think New South Wales is the Promised Land that Abraham was looking for?" I asked.

"Why not?" he said. "I think everyone here is looking for a promised land."

After that, whenever I thought he was too big-headed I teased him by calling him Abraham.

By then we were at the front gate of the Tannery. It was perched on the highest part of Brickfield Hill.

"Oh," I said, "what a grand view of Sydney."

"Haven't you seen it before? Let's stop a minute and have a look."

Before I knew what was happening he was standing behind me pointing over my shoulder to different spots.

"Starting over to the left you can see Cockatoo Island just in front of where the Parramatta river enters the Harbour. On this side of the Harbour is Sydney Cove and then the town starts."

"We're sort of behind the town now, aren't we?"

"Yes. You know where The Rocks are?"

"Oh yes and I can see them just beyond Sydney Cove. They're just down the road from St Philip's Church where the Wilshire's go."

"Do you go there too?"

"Only sometimes … … If I look up the Parramatta River and far away, am I looking at the Blue Mountains?"

"Yes and straight in front of us across the water is the other side of the Harbour. It's called the North Shore."

"Wonder what it's like over there?"

"I'll take you one day. Now look right down Port Jackson towards the sea."

"The coast looks very broken."

"Yep. Little bays and big bays on both sides of the Port, right down to the Heads. Where do you live?"

I pointed over the top of the Government House gardens.

"Woolloomooloo way," he guessed.

"Yes and it's time I was getting back there."

He walked me home, talking all the time about himself and his plans. I wasn't much interested in his blarney but I thought it easier to listen to him than to have him firing questions at me. No-one would know my story until I wanted to tell it. As soon as I reached the garden gate he said he'd see me again and off he went.

Rosy Days

For this patch I'll look for a piece of silk material with colours of the sunset – pale pink through to red.

Will became a fixture in my life. He started strolling past the gate in the late afternoons and striking up a conversation with anyone he saw in the garden. Usually it was the gardener or one of the children. He always asked after me, so Mrs Wilshire soon knew that I had a follower. He appeared on Saturday afternoon and we went off for a walk together. He shortened my name to Cate which I quite liked.

He taught me Sydney. We walked all over, even to the ocean beaches if it was a good day but that was a very long walk. Up the river was a bit easier. He hired a boat one day and took me for a ride to the other side of the Harbour. There wasn't as much going on there as on our side. We explored both sides and watched how the town was growing, criticised new houses we didn't like and cheered buildings we approved. Like me, Will didn't have many friends but he knew lots of people by sight and could strike up a conversation with anyone anywhere. I couldn't. I never worked out how to chat to strangers. Because of him I got to know a few people too.

What was he like, my Will? Well I always thought he was handsome. He was much taller than me – if he dropped his chin onto his chest, the top of my head fitted under it. He had grey eyes, very unusual and very attractive, and light brown wavy hair. He was well built. He stood very straight and was very strong. He had worked hard since he arrived in the Colony and could walk for miles and never feel weary. When he was just a lad living in Bath, he played cricket and was always picked to bat because he could hit the ball so far. In the colony he played some sort of fast, rough football. He could pick me up and swing me around without losing breath at all, but he wasn't allowed those liberties at first! Yes, he became my treasure.

Although he liked to chat, he would sometimes go very quiet. He always noticed if someone was being badly treated. He would help them if he could. He told me how he hated some of the guards he had met, not because they were guards but because they tormented weaker fellows. He was very soft-hearted with children and stopped and talked to any child who looked unhappy. He was always very sure that the future would be rosy. He had no doubts at all about his ability to be successful.

He was proud to tell me that he'd been granted his Certificate of Freedom after only six years at the colony because, he said, he was such a good shoemaker and had firm plans for his future. Mind you, he'd been imprisoned on one of the Thames River hulks for some months before he sailed, so that had something to do with his release date! Will always found the best reason for things that happened to him. He was a true optimist. (I heard that word at the

Wilshire's.)

I told Mrs Wilshire what I knew about him. Will had worked for the Bloomfield family in Liverpool from the time he arrived in the Colony. Mrs Wilshire knew the family. She wrote to Mrs Brookes at Minto and had a very kind letter back from the old lady. She said that her son-in-law had been pleased with Maber's work and that her daughter liked the house shoes made by the young man. They all thought that he would do well as a free man.

"Was there nothing bad about him?" I asked.

"Just one thing. He once beat another convict badly because he'd whipped a native. They say he has a quick temper."

Next time we met I asked Will why he'd been sent to the Colony.

"Stole a cheese, didn't I."

"Is that all you did? Were you hungry?"

"No. Don't much like cheese … I was just so brassed off with life and not being able to do what I wanted, and blocked by all these fancy folk standing in the door of the shop so you can't go in yourself, that I just grabbed the cheese and ran … Got caught straight away. There was a constable standing right outside that shop."

"Oh, Will, that's a stupid story. There must have been something else."

"Nothing worth talking about," was the reply. "Now what about you?"

I wasn't ready to tell Will all of my story. So far he didn't even know my full name. I jumped up and said that I had to get back to work.

"Mrs Wilshire is expecting guests," I said. That wasn't true but I wanted to get away.

When Will leased part of a red brick and shingle property in Kent Street he was very excited. He took me to see it. It was in a big building that had five different sections. At one end was a pub then four houses. The houses were all narrow but had two floors and a basement and went back a long way. There were two rooms on each floor. Will had taken the end house with its front door facing Erskine Street. He paid thirty pounds to lease it for a year, money he had saved before he got his Freedom. It was in a good spot and the house was well separated from the pub.

"Well Cate, what do you think? … Isn't it time we got married? … Would you join me in making the best shoes in Sydney?" He grabbed me and swung me off my feet. I pushed him off.

"Don't get too pleased with yourself," I said. "What makes you think I'd marry you?"

His great smile dropped straight off his face. "I thought you liked me, Cate."

"Maybe I do … a bit … but that's not the same as thinking I'd marry you."

He grabbed me again and tried to kiss me. Up till that afternoon he had been very gentlemanly and never gone further than an arm around my shoulders. I liked him, I really did, and I knew that if he kissed me I'd kiss him back and then what? He still didn't know about Tolson or about Jane. I'd told him very little about the worst parts of my life.

"Cate, I've told you all about my life and the rotten thing that happened to me in Bath and brought me to this place, but you've told me nothing of yours apart from working in a big house in Ireland and looking after a sick child in Dublin. What happened then? You told me about working in a shop in London but the bit of the story between Dublin and that shop you always leave out. You haven't even told me your full name. I want to know it all."

I knew that I had to make a decision. If I told him the lot he might go find someone else to marry. I had a good home with the Wilshire's and some time to wait before I would be free. Maybe Mrs Wilshire would keep me on when my freedom came. I liked Will but once I told him everything I feared he'd gossip about it. I didn't want him telling my story to his football mates. Still, we'd been walking out for weeks. If I wanted to keep him as a friend and perhaps more than a friend, he had to know the rest of my story.

"Let's go to the Rocks where it's sunny. While you watch the ships I'll tell you my story."

We sat facing each other and Will held my hands. I felt very secure talking to him. He watched me all the time and winced at the sad bits about Lizzie and Louisa and Lucy and Tolson. At last I got to my trial and to the terrible New Year at the Factory. I warned him that what was coming was nasty and said that I wanted it always to be a secret.

As I talked about the rape he hugged me as if he was frightened I'd disappear.

"Oh, Cate," he cried, "you're such a little thing, they could've killed you then we'd never have met." He was nearly in tears. "I know this sort of thing happens but you're safe now. I'll take care of you. I'll kill anyone before I'd let them hurt you."

"You don't blame me?"

"No, no! Never."

"You'll never talk about it?"

"I'll never tell anyone." He kissed me gently on the forehead. "I hope they didn't hurt you too much."

I shuddered. "It hurt a lot at the time and then finding I'd have a baby was awful but strangely, my little one's birth was not difficult."

"We've never talked about children but I want to have some one day. What about you?"

"Yes, yes ... I lost my little Jane but I'd like to have another child. You'd be a good Da. You always know how to talk to children. If we have little ones I'll teach them to call me Mam and you'll be Da – that's what I always called my parents."

Will was more upset hearing this tale than I was telling it. I knew then that he was softer hearted than I had guessed and that he would never tell my story or blame me for that awful night. After that day, we never talked again about the most horrible experience of my life. He kept my trust always.

We sat for a long time on the Rocks that day. I explained that because of Tolson I couldn't marry him or anyone. I asked him to see me home then go away and decide what he thought of it all. At the gate he gave me a big, gentle hug.

"Tomorrow is Sunday," he said. "I'll be here by eleven o'clock and wait until you are free, then we'll talk."

That night I didn't sleep much. What would Will make of my story? If we became a couple what would that give me? I knew we'd have to work hard to make a living but I didn't mind that. I hoped that I might have children and was glad that Will felt the same.

I had decided long ago that I wanted to improve myself. Once I was a free person it would be important to shake off the imprint CONVICT that I felt was written on my forehead. I wanted to be seen as the person I had become, not as a person dragging her past behind her. It was like Harriet had said on the ship coming out – the past shouldn't matter.

From Mrs O'Reilly I had learnt the meaning of respect. Everyone at the Manor respected her – even Louisa and her parents. She carried with her a sense that she knew what was the right thing to do in any situation and she always did it. Many of the staff were scared of her. I never knew if any of them were her friends. I learnt that she was my friend and by the time I went to Dublin I knew that she would always be my model. I also found out that from respect comes lasting friendship.

Neither Will nor I had much formal education. The only way I could improve my situation was by reading. Mrs Wilshire had given me permission to read any of the books in her home. Their library included her children's books and several bibles as well as novels written by ladies like the ones Louisa had given me to read. Imagine writing a book. What fun! My writing and spelling would have to improve a bit! Mrs Wilshire also encouraged me to read local newspapers. She explained to me how the Colony was governed and encouraged me to ask questions about anything I didn't understand. I knew I must keep up questioning and learning. I often asked her about new words so one day she took a small book off the shelves and gave it to me. It was a Dictionary that her children no longer needed. She explained how to use it and it helped a lot. Somewhere I still have that little book but it is so well used that it is almost in pieces.

Will wanted to make the best shoes in Sydney and me for his wife. I wanted happiness and his love as well as safety and respect. I saw no reason why these wishes couldn't work well together. I would encourage him to follow his dreams. We would become people of the new world. Sydney people who were proud of their contribution to whatever this country might become.

Finally I slept.

Sunday at last. Mrs Wilshire gave me the full day off so I was ready when Will arrived. We walked down to the Harbour, near Mrs Macquarie's Point, saying nothing much at all but once we sat down he put his arm around me.

"Cate, I want you for my wife. I don't care about going to church and getting certificates and all that stuff, but I know you go to church a bit so perhaps that is important to you." He stopped and looked at me but I didn't say a word. "If it isn't really important then we can decide for ourselves that you are Catharine Jane Maber, and you can come to Erskine Street and we'll make that place our home. Will you take my name and get rid of the one you hate so much that it has taken you months to tell me what it was?"

"Yes, Will."

He sprang to his feet with a real whoop, then gathered me up. The kiss I'd fought off yesterday I was happy to return. My new life had begun. Hand in hand, like a pair of kids, we ran up the hill to the house on the corner of Erskine and Kent Streets. We explored it from top to bottom, deciding what each room would be used for and what furniture we would need. And how did we decide which room would be best for the bedroom? By the oldest test in the world.

Over the next few days I told Mrs Wilshire about Will and me. She had guessed that we were close. She was sorry that we couldn't marry but she understood. She talked to Mr. Wilshire who knew that as long as I stayed in his employ I didn't have to live in their house. This meant that I was free to move to Erskine Street and could continue to work for the Wilshires while Will was getting his business going.

Mrs Wilshire was so good to me. I told her that she was my new Mrs O'Reilly. I had talked a lot about that good woman, so Mrs Wilshire knew how much I respected both of them. She told me that I must never be afraid to talk to her if I was in difficulties. She also gave me a strong brand new purse. "Always keep your money in your own purse, Catharine," she said. "Even though Mr Wilshire and I share everything, we both believe that I should have some money of my own. It has been a good plan. I hope you find it helpful."

Will and I prepared to move in together, using our savings to buy a few bits of furniture and pots for the kitchen. I told him that I wanted to keep some of my own earnings separate from his. He knew how Tolson had robbed me and although he was a bit surprised at us having separate purses, he agreed.

"I won't keep my earnings a secret," I said, "but I want to know how we're spending what we've got. We must share everything, but we each need to have a little bit of money of our own in case of accidents." The day came when we were both glad that I had some savings in my special purse.

In February 1841 I packed my belongings into a carpet bag, a gift from the Wilshires, and with my head held high handed it to Will, who was waiting at the front door. I stepped out into the world as Mrs Catharine Maber. I continued working for Mrs Wilshire but my home was the house on the corner of Erskine and Kent Streets, Sydney Town.

We were very happy. Will had a lot of work mending leather goods and making footwear for the workers of Sydney Town, but his dream of making ladies boots and delicate shoes for special occasions was hard to achieve. People who could afford fancy clothes of any sort had them sent out from England or even America. He made me a lovely pair of fitted shoes, when he'd saved enough of the good leather he bought from Mr Wilshire's tannery. He was careful not to run into debt.

One day, after a visit to the Tannery, he brought home a sheep skin. It was small and very soft. It had come from a lamb and was thought to be too small to be useful. I looked at it for a while remembering the pretty slippers Miss Louisa used to wear in her bedroom. They had been made from fabric but the soft skin gave me the idea of slippers for babies. Maybe the fact that there was a baby on the way made me think of it too! I talked to Will and he told me to use the skin any way I wanted.

Our baby would arrive in the summer. I talked to Mrs Wilshire. She had a little shoe that one of her children had worn. I used it to make a pattern then at home I made two little tubes with a bend for the heel. I put the wool on the inside and stitched the seams with bright colours, using the stitch I had needed when mending Miss Louisa's leather gloves. My bootlets were really cute. I gave Mrs Wilshire a pair and she showed her friends. Any of them who were likely to be grandmothers wanted some too, so I was soon looking for another little sheepskin. Mr Wilshire arranged for us to get any offcuts that were going to waste, or any full skins of very small lambs. I was able to earn a little extra towards our home in Erskine Street but Will insisted that I keep it for myself.

The next thing I did with the sheep skin was to make a new

pouch for Lizzie's button, because the one Miss Louisa had made for me was quite worn out. When I finished the pouch it went into my special purse and there it is today.

Our son was born on 11 February 1842. He was a long, skinny, healthy little boy and his dad thought he was the bonniest baby in the colony. Right from birth his feet were too big for the wee slippers I had made. I put them away in the hope of another baby. Perhaps a little girl some time. He was christened at St Philip's church. We named him William Abraham. By then we both believed that New South Wales was indeed our 'promised land' and that from now on our life would be smooth and happy.

Two Williams in the household was bound to cause confusion, so for my son I used the Irish form of William. I told everyone the baby's name was Liam. Oddly enough, Will never called him anything but Son. He would walk through the house calling "Where's my son?" There was such pride in his voice. Both names fitted our bonny little fellow who was always full of energy.

In May 1842 I got my Certificate of Freedom but continued working for the Wilshires and some of their friends, though now I could pick and choose how much I did. Will and I were truly free to make our own life.

In 1843 Mr Wilshire became the second Mayor of Sydney, which was very exciting for the whole family and created all sorts of extra activities for Mrs Wilshire, so her sister Sarah came to help. I worked at formal dinner parties at least twice a week and there was lots of making and mending to be done. The next year was very busy for both the Mabers and the Wilshires. I was expecting our second child and the Wilshires were leaders of society.

Sarah and I had much pleasure in making sure that Mrs Wilshire's dress for the first ever Mayor's Ball was perfect. The wine red dress, with an enormous hoop and wide neckline, had been sent out from London but it didn't fit as well as we wanted. I had to make many nips and tucks before the great night because Mrs Wilshire was losing weight. She no longer had the energy that had been such a part of her. I began to wonder if something was wrong.

Sarah had a beautiful gown too. Hers was sky blue with lots of lace on the bodice and it was a perfect fit.

On the night of the Ball, Will and I and lots of other people gathered in the centre of George Street outside the Victoria Theatre, to watch all the great people of Sydney arrive. Between us we were able to name many of these folk and we both enjoyed looking at their splendid clothes, though for Will, ladies shoes were still the most interesting.

On September 27 of 1844 our little daughter arrived. I called her Elizabeth in memory of my sister Lizzie. It was also Mrs Wilshire's name. She was very pleased and attended the Christening at St Philip's on 17 November. We always called our little daughter Beth. She was a bonny baby, round and cuddly, not skinny like Liam. Will said she was like me – just the right sized bundle to hold in his arms. He said so many lovely things to me that I never regretted my decision to become Mrs Maber.

Beth had not had her first birthday before trouble came. The whole property we lived in was put up for auction. Until it was sold we were able to stay, paying a weekly rent, but we were worried. When it sold the new owner might not let us stay. For several months we weren't sure what would happen. After the auction the new owner gave us two weeks to get out. He planned to change the place altogether. He might even knock it down. We had to find a new home somewhere that would be in a good spot for Will's business. That was very difficult. Sydney Town was spreading out and rents were increasing all the time. We wondered about moving to the Liverpool district but it was a bit far out. We found a small place just big enough for us to live in, with a corner for Will's tools, and Will got a job at the Tannery while we looked for somewhere better.

While all this was happening I was helping to nurse Mrs Wilshire. She was quite ill. Her sister did most of the work but I helped her, and sometimes stayed in the house at night so that Sarah could have a good sleep. We were already friends and this brought us even closer. Sarah was so lovely with her nieces and nephews that I wasn't at all surprised when she eventually became the second Mrs Wilshire.

Will didn't like his job at the tannery and I didn't like him working there. It was dirty and smelly and the workers ended each day in a local pub. Will joined them, of course. I didn't like the waste of money but I couldn't begrudge him a bit of fun. About a year later he got into police trouble because of a donnybrook *(street fight')* outside that pub. I don't know what it was about but he said he'd been stopping a bully who attacked one of his friends. We had a big row when his name got into the paper. We had to pay a fine and he had to report to the police if he left Sydney.

"How can I hold my head high if you're in police trouble?" I yelled. "Our children need to know the difference between right and wrong and this doesn't help."

"What d'you mean? I did the right thing. I helped my mate."

"If it was right, why did the police grab you?"

"Because him and me were the only ex-convicts there. What we say don't count."

"Oh Will, is that true?"

"Course. Sydney Town has lots of old prison guards in the police force. They have a grudge against ex-cons."

I'd heard this before, but I was still cranky.

"What about the fine? We don't earn enough to give it back to the police. You earned more mending shoes than you do at the Tannery, and you didn't have bullies to put up with."

Will agreed. We stopped fighting and just looked at each other.

"I know," I said. "Leave the Tannery and we'll get your tools out again. We'll live in one room so that you can have a decent work place."

He took some persuading but eventually he agreed. Liam got quite excited because he loved watching his Da work.

Not for the first time I wondered if we should leave Sydney Town. Liam was growing and even at this young age, running wild on the streets. He had some little ragamuffin friends and they were always up to mischief. The other thing I didn't like was the number of sly grog shops everywhere. I quite enjoy a taste of rum for special occasions but the locally made stuff sold at the grog shops was foul. I never touched it but I know that Will did sometimes. I noticed too that my light-hearted, self-confident man was becoming quiet and withdrawn. His hope in the future was dying. He began to look backwards and wonder if his dreams were a waste of time. He was losing faith in himself. I realised that he would always fight for someone else, but not always for himself.

Will often talked about his times with the Bloomfields. Some of the convicts he'd met there had been in the gang that built the road to Goulburn. He'd heard of the Goulburn plains and said he'd like to visit them one day. I began to dream of leaving Sydney and going into the country.

Once I was serving afternoon tea at a party given by Sarah, now Mrs Wilshire. The guests were all ladies who knew me.

"How are things going for you?" one of them asked.

"We're thinking of leaving Sydney."

"Oh really? Where would you go?"

"We're thinking about Goulburn," I said. "Country life would be good for the children and Will knows some people out that way."

This created a lot of chatter and Sarah said she'd miss me. One lady said she'd been to Goulburn.

"What's it like?" I asked.

"The road out there through the mountains is rough and it's only a small town but everyone says it will grow. There's already a big flour mill there which means that the farmers are doing well and I think there is a tannery too."

That was enough for me. I told Will and to my surprise he agreed. Some men he had worked with had gone there when they got their freedom. He might have friends on the Goulburn Plains.

In late summer 1847, Will told the Police we were shifting to Goulburn and I said goodbye to the Wilshire family. Sarah gave me clothes for the children and a copy of one of Jane Austin's books called *Persuasion*. She chose this one because it had been a favourite that we read to each other in the days when we were hemming sheets. She wrote in the front – "Don't forget your friend Sarah. I want to know about your new life." That message was very important to me. I still have the book it is written in. We packed up our home, small though it was, and set out for Goulburn.

Picture a Growing Town

This will be a hard picture. It must show the two rivers and funny houses and the ford we crossed. Part of Auburn Street too.

They tell me that Goulburn is about one hundred and thirty miles from Sydney. Will and Liam set out first and walked every bit of that distance. Liam still remembers it. The road they travelled had many twists because it climbs the mountains, but once over the worst of them it becomes fairly straight and flat. It travels on to Gunning and Yass but we weren't going there.

After we paid for our belongings to go by cart, I had just enough money in my purse for a coach fare to Marulen for Beth and me. Fifteen miles from Goulburn we left the coach where our men were waiting. We walked until it was dark.

It was a beautiful night full of stars and gentle bush sounds. We camped well off the road, ate the bread and cheese I had brought then settled down to sleep. Somewhere near other people were camping too. We could smell the smoke from their fire and then we heard their strange music. Liam told us they had met several native families during their walk and that most of them carried the strange blowing instrument they have. I was never sure what its name was but it was good to hear.

In the morning near our cold fire place, we found a bunch of freshly picked leaves and in the centre one beautiful waratah flower. I think it was a welcome message.

Our journey was nearly over. Goulburn wasn't very far away and we reached it mid-afternoon. Beth rode on Will's shoulders until we crossed the ford over the Mulwaree, then we all joined hands and walked into the town together. The Maber family had arrived.

Goulburn is built between two rivers. They are like arms that hold the town between them. To enter the town we had to cross a ford near the spot where the rivers meet. The rivers are called the Mulwaree and the Wollondilly. Some people say that both of the names come from the native tribes that used to live in the area. They had mostly vanished before we arrived. The main road of the town is called Auburn Street and on or near that road I lived the rest of my life.

Because Will was still bound over from that scrap in Sydney, he had to report in at the Goulburn lock-up straight away. The Police Station was a fairly new building in Sloane Street next to the Court. The prison was behind it hidden by a high wall. I hoped none of us would ever visit that place again.

For a few days we camped near the Mulwaree river while Will and I looked around the town, trying to work out where was the best place to settle. We chose a humpy (I wouldn't call it a house) that was in Auburn Street. We could rent it for two shillings a week.

It was very close to the edge of the road but at the back there was a lovely grassy area where it would be safe for the children to play. It had two rooms with the fireplace outside. It wasn't good enough. I wasn't going to have my children's lives as poor as mine had been. It was time for me to stand tall and save for a bigger house.

I was determined to get as much education as I could for my children. I found out that there was more than one school available but they all charged fees which we couldn't pay yet. In time I located a Dame School that was run by a lady in her own home. I started Liam there straight away and managed to pay the small fee. Liam was a reluctant scholar but I insisted. Both of the children went to Sunday school at St Saviour's, the English church. That helped their reading.

I was equally determined that Will would show the people of Goulburn what good shoemaking was like. There was a tannery in the town so he could get fresh leather for his craft. In the front room of our humpy we soon had the workroom ready for business and in it I displayed a few pieces of my needlework and crochet. It wasn't long before I had people bringing me work and I began looking for a four-roomed house. We could both earn and Liam made a good little messenger boy to fetch and carry for us.

We soon realised that it wasn't going to be easy for Will to make a living for us all by making elegant shoes. Gillespie's Shoe and Boot factory had been in Goulburn for years and a second one opened just after we arrived. Will met Mr Gillespie and the owner of the other factory and, though neither of them offered him a full-time job, Mr Gillespie occasionally called on him to assist with special work. Nonetheless he would probably get more work from mending than making. This was a disappointment.

Liam was certainly keen to learn his Da's trade. He preferred that to his school lessons. I had taught him to read a little but he wasn't very interested, he preferred being with his Da or outside, running and jumping and getting into mischief. He was a gawky kid, tall and energetic. Little Beth, not yet five, was different. She preferred her Mam's company and she enjoyed hearing stories. We used to sing the *Oranges and Lemons* song and *Strawberry Fair* together. She even taught them to her friends. The boys all preferred the *Drunken Sailor* song.

I never taught them *Molly Malone*.

Slowly our life took shape. We moved into a four-roomed house with a work room, a room for us, another for the children and a kitchen with a good fireplace and chimney. Will took a good look at that chimney and said he could rig up a roasting jack like he had seen at the Bloomfields. I knew it would be great if we could have roast meat sometimes. He talked to Mr Gillespie who gave him a couple of strong hooks and a rod to hold the meat. I made a thick plait from string stripped out of a sack that came with us from Sydney, then Will finished the job with a heat shield made from an old tin tray that he attached to legs made out of a pair of forked sticks he found on a gum tree. I began to think that we had found that promised land. We used it for the first time when Will won a piece of mutton at a football match! The jack worked so well that we made sure we took it with us when we moved house.

Every year we celebrated our children's birthdays. Neither Will nor I really knew our own birthdate but we would never forget our children's.

The beginnings of Will's life were sad. He was the second child in the family but early in January of 1815 his three year old brother William died. Two days later Will was baptised and given the same name. We reckoned that my Will must have been born just before Christmas 1814. His Mam, Susanna, died when he was eight and he was barely nineteen when he arrived in the Colony although his records showed that he was twenty.

As for me, I had no idea when I was born. All I know is that when I went to live with my Da at Black Grange Manor, everybody said that I was about eight. From then on I just guessed as well as I could how old I was.

When Liam's eighth birthday arrived, we invited some of his friends for a party. We'd never done this before but for both of us being eight years old seemed to be an important time. We didn't want to see things go wrong for our children. The party was a happy event and made us wonder if we should tell them what it had been like for us when we were that age.

We didn't.

How do you explain a totally different life to children who have only known the free-and-easy ways of a new land? Our two little gems were as carefree and happy as birds in the trees. We didn't want to burden them with our stories.

In the evenings when they were asleep, we spent a lot of time talking about our childhood and I learnt a few things about Will that were new to me. At last he told me what had made him so unhappy that he stole that cheese right under a Constable's nose.

It was quite a long story.

When his mother died, Will was sent to stay with his uncle and aunt in Bathford, a village just a few miles from the City of Bath where he had grown up. His relatives lived half way up Bathford Hill on the corner of a street that led down to the school, so Will went to school most days. He enjoyed his time there and became very fond of his aunt but as soon as he was ten he was sent back to Bath to start training as a shoemaker with his father, John.

They lived in Milk Street. It was close to the dirty, smelly river Avon, used as the drain for the city of Bath as well as for the slaughter-house on Broad Quay. Will's return to his father's home revived his friendship with Joe Parfitt. Will and Joe began playing together when they were little fellows. They were really good mates. They had two favourite games, either throwing sticks into the river hoping to hit a duck or swan, or racing up to the centre of town to look for rich people, who might want someone to hold their horses while they went into the Pump Room near the Abbey, or the Assembly rooms high on the hill.

Once every year, for several months, Bath had lots of visitors. People whose homes were in the towns and villages all over the countryside visited Bath for 'the season'. As Will began to tell me about this, I remembered the book that Miss Louisa gave me called *Northanger Abbey*. I still had that book when I left London but on the ship there was so little to read that lots of people, including some sailors, borrowed it. Also, when we were on deck sewing, either Harriet or I would read the book aloud. We'd often have quite an audience. By the time we got to Sydney Town the book was in pieces and I lost it.

Will told me how he and Joe often earned a few pennies holding horses heads, while handsome young fellows talked to pretty ladies in the street. He told me he began to look carefully at their boots because they were quite different from those his father made. He talked to John about what he was seeing and his father explained about the cost of leather, and the need to make shoes and boots that would suit people working in the country. He encouraged Will to watch and learn about more expensive styles but warned him not to imagine that they could produce boots like those the rich people wore.

Will wasn't put off.

"I made up my mind then and there that one day I'd make beautiful shoes and boots, and I began to draw sketches of what I saw on the ladies' and the gentlemen's feet. We earnt lots of pennies holding horses' heads. Young fellows would ride slowly up the streets. If they saw some pretty girl they knew, they'd leave the horse with one of us and walk off with her. Joe always talked about the smart coats and shirts the men wore but I was more interested in their boots and the ladies shoes."

"I suppose you looked at the ladies rosy cheeks too," I teased.

"Not really ... Do you know it was then that I saw that the gentry wore shoes fitted to each foot. The two shoes of a pair were different just as a pair of feet are different."

"Oh yes, Will. I first noticed that when I worked for Miss Louisa. My clogs looked so clumsy next to her shoes but our feet were about the same size."

"You are clever, Cate. You saw it too. I kept this knowledge in my head and dreamed about the day I'd leave my Da and finish my Journeyman training with a new Master."

As soon as Will finished training with John, he moved out of home to work with another craftsman for a while, so that he would be qualified as a Journeyman Shoemaker. His mate Joe lived with his father, Silas Parfitt, in Peter Street and was apprenticed to shoemaker Henry Vaughan. Will moved around to Peter Street where he shared a room with Joe. I'm not sure whether Will was working with Parfitt or Vaughan. One of them was his new master. He soon completed his training so was now a Journeyman and entitled to work towards joining the Guild.

Entry to the Guild was carefully controlled and before he could apply he had to complete one or more master work pieces.

While Will looked at people's feet, his mate Joe looked at their clothes. He was fussy in his dress and was determined to 'be a toff'. He didn't care about shoes at all. He and Will often argued about what was more important – shoes that got wet, muddy and dirty on the pavements or a coat that showed off a man's shoulders and straight back.

They were about seventeen years old. Kids squabbling for the sake of it but still friends.

Will's habit of sketching shoes and boots people were wearing, meant that he had lots to talk to his Master about. He talked to Henry and Silas and his Da, showing them that there was a new fashion. They agreed that what he said was true but none of them was willing to give him permission to use their precious leather stocks to experiment with the new shape of shoes.

Will needed to find someone to make a shaped pair of shoes, for someone who would help him pay for the leather. He tried Joe, telling him that this is what the toffs were wearing. Joe was totally disinterested and told Will he had better things to do with his money than chase rainbows.

Will knew that if he could produce a beautiful pair of ladies shoes they could, perhaps, be his first master work for admission to the Guild. He just needed help to pay for the right leather.

Will thought of his aunt and decided that next time he had a day off, he'd visit her and suggest that he make her a pair of the latest style of shoes. He told Joe of his plans and asked to borrow his coat. He wanted to make a good impression on his aunt.

"No way," said Joe. "You're bigger'n me … you'd bust the seams. If you want a fancy coat, go buy one." The coat cost Joe two shillings and sixpence. Will didn't have that much. He didn't argue but he asked again. Joe agreed that he wouldn't need his coat on the day Will wanted it but he wasn't happy about it being borrowed. He kept talking about charging for a loan.

When the day came Joe was out, so Will picked up the coat, told Silas that he was going to see his aunt, and took off up Walcot Street to Bathford. It was a beautiful day and Will enjoyed the three mile walk. Most of the time he carried the coat but he made sure it was on before he knocked at his aunt's door.

His aunt and uncle were pleased to see him.

"Come in, come in," they said. "You do look smart. Let's have a cup of tea and hear all about life in Bath." The visit started very well.

"I'm a Journeyman, now, aunt, and I plan to work towards being admitted to the Guild."

"Goodness gracious me," said his uncle. "What do you have to do to manage that?"

"I have to make something special and I plan to try something

VERY special for a lady."

Uncle laughed. "Sounds as if you need to talk to your aunt. I'll go out and put stakes up against my broad beans."

His aunt was curious. "What are you talking, about?" she asked.

Will told her. He explained how really good shoes must be made to fit each foot and that if they were special, then they would be made of fine, soft leather, and probably have a pattern on them. She was very puzzled until he showed her some drawings he had made of what he saw on ladies feet in Bath.

"Could you do something like that for me, Will?"

"I'd like to try."

She took her shoes off and Will removed his jacket so that he could kneel down and draw outlines of her feet on a piece of paper.

Suddenly there was a loud knock at the door.

"Open up! Open up! Police."

Will's aunt screamed and his uncle came running in from the garden. He opened the door and there stood Joe with Constable George Thatcher.

Joe pushed into the room. "There, you see, officer," he yelled. "That's my coat. He stole it."

"I didn't, I didn't," shouted Will. "You knew I wanted to borrow it and you knew where I was going."

There was a terrible row.

"I refused to lend it and he took it without permission. He stole it. Give it back!" Joe yelled.

Will picked up the coat and threw it at Joe.

"Take it, you mongrel," he shouted.

Joe missed the catch and the coat dropped to the floor.

Joe screamed again. "The coat's ruined. I'll get you for this." He aimed his fist at Will. The boys danced out into the street with the Constable trying to separate them.

Several neighbours heard the rumpus and came out to watch the fun, while Will's aunt and uncle hung their heads in shame. What a disgrace to have a police arrest on their doorstep.

The constable got control of Will, marched him back to Bath and then to the lock-up at Shepton Mallet. Joe skipped off home, glad that he'd won the fight and pleased that he wouldn't have to share his room with Will any longer. Their friendship was over.

Not long after Will fronted the Assizes at Taunton. Joe gave evidence against him and Will was sentenced to four months in goal, the first week was in solitary confinement because he had yelled so much abuse at Joe during the hearing.

"I think I lost faith in friendship after that," said Will as he finished the story. "Both Joe and Silas knew that I only wanted a loan of that coat but neither of them would tell the magistrates. When I came out I went back to live with my Da, but I couldn't settle to work and he blamed me and my high ideas for all the trouble. I felt that my time in jail had put a mark on me that would never go away. I would never be allowed to join the Guild. I felt so desperate that I didn't care what happened to me."

He was so sad he stopped talking and hid his face in his hands.

"So that's why you stole the cheese when a Constable was watching?" I asked gently.

"Yes, I suppose so." He sounded uncertain. I still wasn't sure that I had the full story.

No, we wouldn't tell our children. Let's keep their life light-hearted and happy, free of our disappointments and sadness.

Gold Dust Isn't Golden

The 1850s had begun. A crazy time. Gold rushes and visitors everywhere. Now I must stitch stick figures of men pushing crazy wheelbarrows along a dusty road.

Goulburn had never been busier as men, both in groups and alone, marched through the town one way or came limping back the other. Some told tales of fortunes made and lost, others said nothing. Others were off to bring their families up to the fields because they were sure they had chosen a good spot for the next dig. Tales were told of villainy and murder, of kindness and help. I only listened with half an ear. The ones who thought finding gold would be easy reminded me of Tolson – stars in front of their eyes and no brains behind them!

Will had stars in front of his eyes too but fortunately not about gold. It was summer. Cricket was being played and he was about to show his son how to bat and bowl. His brains were working well. He listened to the talk but never showed any interest in following the streams of ragged men on their way to make a fortune. Sometimes I teased and said it was because he had put on weight and lost his energy but I knew that wasn't true. We had agreed that we could do better by growing up with Goulburn. We planned to take our place here as respectable, hardworking people instead of racing off after every new idea. We wanted the 'promised land' to come true for Liam and Beth.

I moved the children into our room and used their room to offer overnight accommodation to men who were off to the gold fields, but who had enough in their pockets to pay for a meal and a good night's rest. Our first lodgers became part of our family. John and Mary Surrey weren't chasing gold. Just as we put up our LODGINGS sign they arrived in town and needed somewhere to stay. Ann was their only child then and they lived with us for a few weeks. We never lost touch. Their second daughter arrived later and we went to the Catholic church to see both little girls baptised. My Beth enjoyed playing 'little mother' to the girls and a few years later, when Mary died, Ann spent more and more time with us. Ann was like a second daughter.

Every little bit of money I could add to what Will earned made us safer. This was very important because one thing worried me a lot. I felt that Will's eyesight wasn't as good as it needed to be for his work. Actually I wasn't sure if it was his eyes or his hands. Sometimes they seemed to shake. He had a few nasty accidents with the awl and needed Liam or me with him whenever he began to sew leather. He clearly had difficulty threading the needle as well as positioning the awl. He wouldn't admit it but I was sure there was a problem.

It was about now that Will started going off at the weekends exploring the countryside. He started off by following the Wollondilly which was the bigger of the two rivers that bounded Goulburn. The Mulwaree ran through such flat country as it reached Goulburn that it didn't look very interesting. The Wollondilly took him through the hills towards the Crookwell district. He wasn't looking for gold but for a few ex-convicts who had come this way when they were free. He started wandering to nearby settlements to see if he could find any of them. He went to Grabben Gullen where he heard there were sapphires in the river. He didn't find any mates or any sapphires so wandered on to Gunning where he met up again with a fellow called Foley.

As well as looking for friends, Will was interested in the bush itself. He watched birds and became quite good at imitating the sounds they made. Once he found a small pink and grey parrot with a broken leg. He brought it home, mended the leg and the pretty little thing lived in and around our house for about a year. Then a friend came calling and they flew away together.

If there were flowers in bloom Will always come home with a bunch for me. I liked the beautiful waratah but his favourite was the wattle and I loved it too, though it did make me sneeze! He especially liked the district called Taralga (what a funny name) but I was relieved that he didn't want to move us out of Goulburn to a smaller town like Gunning or Crookwell, even though at Gunning he had met a friend. He always seemed more interested in the countryside than the people and occasionally he'd bring home a rabbit. If it was young I cooked it on the roasting jack but old ones were best if I put them in a soup. It was good free food.

Disaster struck in February 1852. Will had gone over to Gunning to visit that Foley fellow. They went to Bartley's Inn and had a few then settled down for the night in Foley's humpy. Next morning all hell broke loose as the pair of them were arrested for having spent the night breaking into a house and stealing money and guns. They were both taken to Yass to be identified. By the time I had persuaded Mr Walsh, the lawyer, to speak for Will Foley had been turned loose while Will was charged and brought to Goulburn jail. You know, I never had a bill from Mr Walsh – he said it was *pro bono*. It took me several years to find out what that meant but since he didn't save Will I didn't think he should have expected payment from me anyway!

The trial was held in Goulburn just eight days after the robbery. It was a put-up job if ever I saw one. I had about two minutes with Will before it began and he told me he had not been involved. I believed him. He had a horror of jail and the sort of things that happen there.

There were other reasons why I was sure that he hadn't been involved. He hated guns and we had never had one in the house. He was also supposed to have stolen a saddle and pieces of horse harness. What was he supposed to have done with them? At the trial no one could suggest what he had done with the stuff he was supposed to have stolen. None of it was ever found. Of course he was innocent but he didn't win. Some sneaky child hiding under the bed said it was him. All the kid could see in that dark room was a bit of an upside-down face and a cabbage tree hat. Yes, Will had such a hat but so did everyone else in the Colony. Anyway, the hat was found and identified but it belonged to Foley and Foley had been let off!

What a disaster, my husband sentenced to five years on the roads. He'd never been on the roads and I was scared of what might happen to him if he was in a chain gang. Luckily, the first thing that happened was that he was sent to Cockatoo Island for assessment – whatever that meant.

Heavy sorrow was on me as I saw him marched out of Goulburn in chains. Not since the day at the Manor when I heard my Da had left me, had I felt so alone. I had two children to keep safe and no certainty of when I'd see Will again. *'Help me Mrs O Reilly'* I cried. Her reply was clear: *'Talk to Sarah.'*

What good advice. I had enough money in my special purse for a coach fare to Sydney. I sent a message to Mrs Wilshire with a copy of the newspaper report of Will's trial, telling her I was coming to see her.

Leaving the children in the care of John and Mary Surrey, I went to Sydney and visited my kind friend. She was lovely and I stayed with her for two nights. We talked about the affair for a long time.

"What will you do for money?" she asked.

"I already rent a room to lodgers but now I'll make space for a bed in the workroom and take in more. I already have some needlework customers so I'll just look for others."

Mr Wilshire remembered Will and me and he talked to me so kindly, telling me that I could apply for a Ticket-of-Leave for Will after he had served part of his sentence. He said that I would need a lawyer's help but that it could be done.

Before I left Sydney I visited the Rocks where Will and I used to sit. I looked across the water to where he was. The island looked as forbidding as always only now I could see human figures moving around. I hoped that one was Will and that he knew I was there. He was so close and yet I couldn't see him.

Sarah told me to keep in touch and I carried away clothes for both the children, some of Sarah's old dresses for me and all sorts of other gifts that would help us on the way. When I got home, hidden in a pocket I found an envelope that contained a pre-paid coach ticket for Sydney that I could use at any time. What a good friend!

Several of Will's friends visited me, mostly from the shoe business or people he'd got yarning to somewhere, sometime. One of these strangers brought me a rabbit that I shared with Mary Surrey. Hector Dallas, another bootmaker, tried to be helpful but he was one of those sort of fellers who make a hames of everything he does. He came the day Liam and I were hanging a hessian curtain to divide the workroom. He insisted on helping. He cut the rope too short, tried to dig a hole in the wall instead of using the beam to hang it from, and finally fell off the box he was standing on, landed on my foot and knocked himself out. It was a long time before I accepted his help again.

Foley, from Gunning, didn't put in an appearance. Just as well. I'd have called him a gobshite or worse. It wouldn't have been good for the children to hear language like that coming out of my mouth.

I gave up trying to get Liam to school. Now ten years old my son was already doing some small shoe mending work. He also earned many pennies taking messages for people, or doing other odd jobs. He was very serious about his role as man of the house and I noticed that he often told people that his name was William, not Liam.

I was able to offer dressmaking, mostly alterations, as well as knitting and crochet. I also began to look for occasional work as a maid. Beth's job was looking after our kitchen and keeping the space we rented out to travellers in good order. She attended school as much as possible. It was tough but we managed. I made sure that the children knew that Will was not guilty and told them to hold their heads up high if anyone made remarks about him.

"Never, even for one second, think that he might be guilty," I said. "It doesn't matter what anyone says to you. Just remember that your Da didn't do this."

Winter was very wet that year so keeping our stone house warm and dry was a constant problem. Liam was so good. He went out every day scouting for firewood. Another job I didn't have to do.

One wet day he came home very excited.

"Mam, Mam, come and see. Mulwaree's in flood. Got to go watch." He whirled through the house and out the back door and disappeared while Beth and I just stared.

"We're not going," I said. "No point in the whole family getting wet!" We settled by the fire and I continued the knitting lesson I was giving her.

Liam was gone most of the day. He finally arrived home with mud from head to toe and laughing as he talked. "Oh Mam, you and Beth should have come. People on other side were screaming for help as the river rose near their doors. No one had a boat and most of the horses wouldn't go near the river. You know old Mr Craig, the coffin maker, well he got me to go up to his shop and help him carry one of his coffins down. 'This'll float' he said! What a joke! We put it in, pushed it out and it went straight down! Several ladies said they were glad it sank because they wouldn't want to be saved by a coffin. Oh, Mam, all these grown-ups behaving like little kids." He stopped to catch his breath then started again. "There were two men who could swim so when a really long coil of strong rope was fetched from the Mill they swam over with it and persuaded two or three younger people to hold on and they were pulled across, but it was slow going. At last the grumpy butcher, Sam Davis, let a couple of fellows bring his huge meat vat down. They tied rope around it, pulled it over, filled it with people and pulled it back to safety."

By now, little mother Beth had poured all our hot water into the tin bath on the floor by the fire and I was able to peel off Liam's filthy clothes and get him into it. He chuckled long and loud then started talking again. "You know Mam, the funniest thing wasn't noticed by anyone but me. On the other side, up near the tree line, the Aboriginal family visiting to catch eels, were watching and laughing. They pointed at the silly things that were happening. They weren't worrying about the water rising and I reckon they thought we were all mad not to do as they did. Just light a fire and wait for the rain to stop and the water to go down … You know, I think they'll make a dance about it."

"Like a 'Crobree'?" asked Beth. "I think that'd be great too." She always believed what her big brother said.

I think that flood gave a lot of people a fright. Everyone began to talk seriously about the need for a bridge. Eventually they built the Fitzroy Bridge over the Mulwaree close to the ford that we had crossed when we arrived.

Our year had started badly but by October the view wasn't so gloomy. When I arrived in the colony, Cockatoo Island was a huge bare rock in the harbour. Since then someone had decided that it could be made useful. Part of it became a barracks for the navy and part of it a prison. Holes in the rocks became secure stores for crops grown in the colony. There was an incident at the Island and my Will was a hero. It was in the papers. I got copies of what was written and read the accounts to the children so that we would all tell the right story to our nosy friends and neighbours. Will could have died. The stored wheat in those rock silos nearly killed him but finally helped him to freedom.

A group of prisoners had been sent into a deep hole to empty the grain stored there. It had been left too long, got a bit damp and begun to rot. The smell was frightful. The men began to cough and splutter but were told:

"Stop the fuss and get on with it."

First one then another collapsed. A senior officer arrived and told the guards to pull the men out. Will was one who collapsed. Out in the fresh air, Will recovered and insisted on going back into the rock silo *not once but twice* after he'd got out. Will helped save those who had been overcome by the fumes from stale grain. It was such big news that Will and a couple of others were rewarded by having their sentences reduced. Will was given an eight months reduction.

Mr. Wilshire had told me that I could apply for a Ticket-of-Leave for Will. As his wife I was entitled to do this so it was time to get started. It took nearly two years but I certainly learnt a lot doing it.

It's worth a whole new patch.

Legal Matters

Now for a patch that will be like a page of writing. Some letters and a quill pen with a bottle of ink.

I went first of all to Mr Walsh who had been the Defence lawyer when Will was before the courts. Mr Walsh was the Chief Clerk of the Court and the Keeper of the Court Records. I told him that I wanted to apply for a Ticket-of-Leave for Will so that I could get him home.

He looked very sober and said that it wouldn't be possible. "The Government entertains a decided objection to prisoners holding a ticket-of-leave for the Districts in which they were convicted."

He chanted this statement in such a sing-song voice that at first I thought he was joking. I smiled and nearly laughed but he shook his finger at me and assured me that this was no joke.

I heard that statement so many times over the next two years that I learnt it by heart. In the end I felt like joining in with whoever was saying it! In the end, of course, I saw it in writing but in the end I won! I brought Will home.

"If you want a ticket then move out of Goulburn," he snapped. "You will never get one while you are living here." He waved his hand to dismiss me. As I turned to leave his office I heard Mrs O'Reilly's voice:

'Stand tall.'

I stopped, turned around, grabbed hold of the back of a chair for support and spoke to the top of the man's bent head.

"Mr Walsh ... I'm determined to apply for a Ticket and I'll not leave Goulburn. I can't afford to shift my family and I'm well known here and can earn a living to keep us all. You tell me I won't get one but I will try. Mrs Wilshire told me I'm entitled to do so. I need you to tell me how to do it."

He looked absolutely amazed that I had challenged him. In a very nasty voice he replied: "And who is this Mrs Wilshire who knows so much?"

"Mrs Wilshire is my friend. Her husband was the second Mayor of Sydney. He explained about it to both of us."

Mr Walsh's eyes opened right up. He put his pen down and turned and looked out the window for several minutes.

"Well ... you might be entitled to apply but it'll be a waste of money and effort. You won't succeed. Why do you want to do it? What makes you think it's worthwhile?"

"Anything is worth doing to get my husband free. You defended him. You know he wasn't guilty of the charge that put him on Cockatoo and I know that too. As his wife I'm entitled to apply for a Ticket. Will and I like Goulburn, we want to bring up our children here. I want my husband back home."

Mr Walsh fiddled with his pen again and looked at me as if he wanted to work out what I was made of. Finally he replied.

"I will do nothing unless you can get at least six good references from people in Goulburn who know you and who support your story that you are well-known and that your work will enable you to support your family."

"But what sort of people should I ask?"

"That's your problem. If you're so well-known you'll work it out." In a very nasty voice he added, "Go away and don't return till you have the names of people who agree to support your application. You'll also have to work out how to pay my fee. No more *pro bono,*" were his last words.

That night I sat down with the children and told them what we had to do to get Da home. I asked them to keep what we were doing a secret but to think hard about important people in Goulburn who knew us. They were eight and ten years of age and in the way of children everywhere, they knew most of the people by name. They also knew which people were pleasant and which ones weren't; which ones said "Hello!" and which ones pushed them off the footpaths.

I also knew people I had worked for and who had recommended me on to their friends. I was sure that we could find six people.

It wasn't as easy as I thought. Some people were away, some didn't want to have anything to do with the law. Some were so busy, or so grand, that when I tried to see them I had to wait weeks before I could get an appointment. None the less, after about a year I was able to go back to Mr. Walsh with my six names. He was stunned. It was clear that he had never expected to see me again and when he saw the names on my list he started to treat me more politely. He even invited me to sit down. He then told me what preparation of the Petition would cost. It was a lot of money, so I said I'd work for him or his wife if we could trade my work skills for his. He sneered at first but a few days later he sent a message that I should see his wife. I had worked for her before so I was able to arrive at an agreement that would cover most of my costs, though it meant working for her as both maid and needlewoman for a very long time.

Who were the people who gave me a reference?

Mr Hy Roach JP, a landowner over Gunning way. (That's a funny Christian name. I think it was probably Humphrey, but I never knew. It was always written as Hy.)

R Waugh was the Coroner. Dr Robert Waugh was a very well know man. He invented Baking Powder!

H Laverley. The children gave me his name. He was a kind man.

J Chatfield. I talked to Lieut William Chatfield about a reference. He agreed to do it. I don't know why the petition was signed by J Chatfield.

William Ross. This man was a Reverend in the Presbyterian Church. I sometimes attended his services because they sang the hymns that I knew. He was happy to help me. He lived in a lovely house in Craig Street close to his church. Before I knew he was a Reverend, I used to stop and talk to him and his wife when I walked by, if they were busy in their pretty garden.

Patrick Plunkett. Captain Plunkett was a Police Magistrate in Goulburn so he ran the Police as well as sitting on court cases. He was a busy man.

Why did they help me? Some knew me because I had worked in their homes – helping with dress-making or curtain making, or providing proper service at table when they had dinner parties. Some had used my services to provide accommodation for their acquaintances. Some knew Will because he was interested in cricket and had been showing Liam and his mates how to play the game. At least one had always said that Will wasn't guilty. Liam found that out from his little mates. Children always gossip about what their parents are saying.

For their own reasons these people agreed to help. I didn't see what they said for ages but when I did they were all good. I saw the petition before it went to Sydney and I couldn't believe it. The language was so flowery and strange. The part with the references was easy to read but the other stuff … I can't describe it because a lot of it I had trouble understanding. Such words! Such long sentences! I suppose that is why lawyers are such busy people – they have to learn to write in a different language.

As well as the words, the writing was beautiful. It was done by a man who made a living by writing documents for the Courts or letters for ordinary people. He wrote a letter to Will for me to tell him that a Petition was being prepared. Later on I got to know him quite well

The petition for a Ticket-of-Leave went to Sydney in March 1854, I was told in July that it had been successful and on 22 September the Ticket was granted for Goulburn and Will came home. That was all I cared about.

Life is Multi Coloured

For this patch I'll look for a piece of material with mixed colours and no particular pattern

Will was home, the children, now twelve and ten, were growing up and we were part of Goulburn. The town was changing all the time. The Church of England opened St Nicholas' church in North Goulburn so I made contact with them. It was closer than St Saviour's, the other English church, and by now I almost understood their services. Both of the children had been baptised in the Church of England in Sydney so it seemed the sensible thing to do. Sometimes we would go as a family to special services held at St Nicholas. Harvest Festival or Christmas were favourites. Will made contacts that way to help him with his junior cricket team and Liam, who learnt the game from his dad, was soon leading it.

The two years Will was on Cockatoo finished my hopes for Liam's education. He had been the man of the house and did not want to be a child again. He told me that though I might go on calling him Liam, for all other people he was William.

"I'm not Irish," he said, "I'm part of this new place."

I was a bit hurt at first but I accepted his decision. There were times when my Irish accent gave people an excuse for being nasty. He had a point.

Even though she did a lot of housework during those two years, I was very pleased that Beth still managed to attend Mr Senden's day school in North Goulburn. He never charged me full fees, because Beth cleaned the classroom every morning and each year I made a set of pinafores for the girls' class.

As well as cricket, Liam learnt a lot about his trade from his Da but he didn't want to work with him. Gillespie's Shoe and Boot making factory was the place to be. Will knew this was sensible. He had met old man Dennis Gillespie soon after we arrived in Goulburn and sometimes, over the years, worked for Dennis or his son Charles, another keen cricketer. As soon as he could, Liam was apprenticed there. He had regular pay and didn't have the problem of waiting for work. The factory produced shoes for sale in the *emporium*, and in due course Will ended up mending them! That made us all laugh.

Those same two years marked Will permanently. His eyesight was now very poor for close work, and his experience in the silos on Cockatoo left him with a dread of closed spaces. He was happiest when he was outdoors. It was well that I continued to take in lodgers, and that a number of people hired me regularly to provide service at their big dinner parties. My earnings were more regular than Will's.

I was glad he was involved with cricket though sometimes I thought he took this interest a bit far. If work was slow, he got into the habit of rolling up a swag and wandering off for days at a time, visiting other small towns in the area and spreading the word about starting junior cricket teams. He re-visited Crookwell and Yass and it must have been cricket that took him once to Young. He got a lift with a carter for most of the one hundred miles, but why go so far just to try to get a team going? I was never sure if that was what he was really up to, but he always came home with good tales to tell about what he had seen and who he had met and he always had bush flowers for me. The time he went to Young he brought me cherries.

As time passed I often met some of the people he met on these trips. They would pop in and say hello if they were in Goulburn on business and one or two even lodged with us occasionally.

Once he came home carrying a long trailing piece of creeper with white flowers like stars. He had pulled it up and there were roots on part of it. We popped it in the ground and looked after it a bit and it grew and grew. First of all it stayed on the ground but one piece reached the corner of the house and went straight up. I found out that it was called clematis. Soon I was giving roots to anyone who wanted them.

I liked a good walk too. Sometimes I'd take off early in the morning to beat the boundaries of Goulburn, look at the gardens, have a sticky-beak at new houses and generally watch how this place was growing. Big buildings were going up like that huge *emporium* on the corners of Auburn and Montague streets. It was a big, dark shop but it sold everything except food. There was material for clothes and household goods as well as ready-made garments for working people. You could buy ribbon or tape by the yard and it sold buttons and press studs and hooks-and-eyes and wool by the skein and ... I used to like walking around and looking at what it was possible to buy, even if I didn't have the time to do anything with it or the money to buy it!

Mandelson's built a fine red brick hotel in Sloane Street. It was the place where wealthy or important people stayed when visiting

Goulburn. I used to stand outside and dream about my little Beth going and working there one day. It was the hotel with the best reputation in Goulburn.

Elegant houses were going up in Grafton Street. One that the children liked was where the Marwick's lived. The red brick house wasn't big but behind it was a large empty field. That was where the circus camped when they came into town about once a year. No wonder the children liked to wander down there! I liked the beautiful bright red letter-box that was placed near the front of that house. It was very tall and I wondered why, until I was walking there one morning and saw a gentleman on his horse post a letter without getting off. Huh, I thought, the gentry like to be lazy and even letter-boxes help them!

The house I liked best was built of stone and brick. It was on the other side of the road to the letter-box and had a back yard dipping down towards the Mulwarree. It had a high pitched roof with attic rooms up there. It started off as a private home but it changed and became a hotel, probably because there was space behind it for horses to graze while their owners were relaxing.

Goulburn was becoming a fine and important place. There was even talk that we would soon be able to send messages by the telegraph, though I didn't quite understand what that meant.

Sometimes, I'd think of childhood walks sister Lizzie and I enjoyed before she died. Now, on the other side of the world, I'd walk to the Mulwaree Ponds, as the river was known, and sit and make daisy chains from the flowers I found. It was while I was there that I saw my first duck-billed platypus. I'd heard about them and I wasn't sure that I quite believed the story. Will saw them years ago. He said you needed to be quiet if they were around. One afternoon I was dreaming about Lizzie and there was a splash right near my feet. I started watching and there were two of them ducking and diving and chasing each other around. It was such a pretty sight. I told Will and we started going down there in the evening to see what we could see. While the river was flowing and there was water in the ponds they were always there. In time those play mates gave me the courage to ask Will about Young.

Telegraph arrived in 1858. The new Post Office building wasn't ready for it so it was installed in a special room at Mandelson's Hotel. I even remember the year because something amazing happened. I was sent one of the first messages that came to Goulburn! I was scared when the envelope arrived. Will was there and he opened it for me. It was from Sarah Wilshire. It was a very short message. "Please visit very soon." We were both surprised.

"That's nice," said Will. "You could do with a holiday but how are you supposed to get there?"

I thought a bit.

"I know," I said. "Mrs Wilshire gave me a ticket for the coach when you were on Cockatoo. I have it hidden in a safe place."

Little Ann Surrey was living with us at the time, and she and Beth chimed in, "You go, Mam. We'll do the cooking."

I found the ticket; I booked onto the coach then, with Will by my side, walked proudly down Sloane Street and into Mandelson's and sent a message back. "Next Wednesday."

When I arrived in Sydney I was met by one of the older Wilshire daughters. The family had just moved to a new house in Wylde Street, so she was there to guide me to it. Once we arrived I found great excitement in the Wilshire home.

First of all I had to be shown all over the new house and garden. It was really grand. The house was built of stone and looked out towards the harbour. It had two levels plus a big cellar for keeping stores. There were lovely curtains at all the windows, and an excellent kitchen with a very modern oven. The garden had vegetables and lots of flower beds as well. It reminded me of The Manor where I had worked so many years before.

One room had been set aside as a sewing room. The older girls were as excited as their mother when they took me into it. They all talked at once as they showed me a magic machine they now had. It was a treadle sewing machine. It needed feet to turn it while hands guided cloth under the needle. Pieces of material could be sewn together in no time at all.

I couldn't believe that such a thing existed and I was very puzzled that they had brought me to Sydney to show me something I could never use. Sarah left the girls playing with the machine and took me through to her morning room. We sat down to have a cup of tea together and she told me the story.

Mr Wilshire had an agent in America who bought him equipment for his factory and anything else that he needed that wasn't available in the colony. Over the years they had done a lot of business together. Mr Wilshire had recently asked the agent to get him some new equipment for the factory and to look into the possibility of one of the new sewing machines for ladies.

Some weeks ago a ship had arrived with Mr Wilshire's order. It had included two sewing machines as well as the equipment for the factory. The agent's letter suggested that Mr Wilshire might like to offer the second machine for sale. That made Mr Wilshire very cross. He wasn't going to be an agent for a person who was his agent! He said that he would neither sell it nor pay for it and his wife and daughters could do with it what they pleased. The ladies of the house decided very quickly. The second machine was for me but first I had to stay in Sydney and learn how to put it together and how to use it. Sarah told me that Mr Wilshire had already sent a telegraph to Will, letting him know that they were keeping me in Sydney for a full week.

When I realised what this would mean to me I began to cry. I knew that with such a machine I could get lots of work. It wouldn't matter if Will didn't earn very much. I could keep our family and wouldn't have to work in other people's homes so much. How would I ever be able to thank the Wilshire family?

I spent a week with them and once I could handle the machine I did a whole lot of mending that had been waiting. I also made a new pair of sheets and pillow-slips for Sarah's bed. Oh it was good to give something back to those kind people. Mr Wilshire organised a carrier to take the machine to Goulburn and I went back on the coach, with working shirts for my men, pretty new dresses for Beth and Ann and warm skirts for me, all selected from clothes the Wilshire's had grown out of. In no time at all the machine reached me and I was in business.

Beth was growing up and when she reached twelve she thought she should leave school, but I made her stay for another year. I wanted her to be much better educated than anyone else in the family. She wasn't tough like her brother or me. She had all the gentleness and dreaminess of her Da – the gentleness and dreaminess that sometimes led him into odd situations, like the one at Young which I never understood. I don't think he did either.

Young. I don't want to think about it yet. I'll get to it later.

While Will explored the bush and found out about wallabies and wombats, I walked the roads and lanes and fields of Goulburn. It was the way I kept in touch with those who had helped me get Will's Ticket. I wasn't pushy but I always said a polite "Good morning, Sir," if I met any of them. Walking also helped me get to know other people, some of whom might be land owners or have homes in town. That is how, when I got stuck in the river, I was rescued by friends.

One day I decided to go over Thorn's Crossing to pick mushrooms that I knew should be up on the other bank. The Mulwaree was deeper than usual and flowing fast. While I was thinking about it one of my friends came up. He was a big strong fellow who grew beautiful vegetables in his garden and sometimes gave me a few.

"You wanna' cross?" he said. "I'll give you a piggy-back."

"What fun," I said. "Haven't had a piggy-back since my Da gave me one."

We set out and reached half way when my friend slipped off the crossing and we were both floundering in deep, rushing water. I thought I'd drown and didn't know how Will would manage without me. Suddenly, I felt myself dragged out of the water and perched on the saddle in front of a man on horseback. That horse took us back to safety with my piggy-back friend hanging onto the rider's leg. Once we were safe, the horse turned again and galloped off before anyone said a word.

The fellow on the horse was another of my friends. Well, not really! He was a farmer down Braidwood way and as well he had a fine two storey brick house in Grafton Street. It had iron lace on both the balcony and downstairs on the verandah, and it had a lovely garden. One morning, when he was busy pruning a rose bush, I stopped to admire the beautiful flowers. I thought he was the gardener. We had quite a chat and he gave me the last bloom on the bush. I never knew his name.

It was a pity this rescue story got into the newspaper but it was a bit of a laugh. Think of me stuck mid-stream and he on his horse picking me up and carrying me across. Will wasn't amused but the kids, now nearly grown up, thought it was a great joke. Somebody said it was just like Lochinvar at the wedding. I wasn't sure what that meant till Beth told me about the old Scottish tale in a poem she'd learnt at school – a bride stolen away by a man on a quick horse.

"What rubbish!" I said, but for a few days it was the talk of the town.

Will certainly wasn't amused!

"You talk about holding our heads high. How can I if my wife knows people I've never met? Rich people … … People who live in smart houses and have good horses … People who give my wife roses and carry her in their arms."

That made me mad.

"If I didn't make it my business to talk to people I'd never have got you off Cockatoo. My head is always high even if someone tells me you're drunk again! Nothing I do will ever shame you or make you drop your head!"

We had a bitter row and weren't friends for quite a few days but we got over it. Mostly we were a happy and contented couple. The story in the paper that Will threw a cup of hot tea at me wasn't true. No matter what anyone says, it simply wasn't true. I dropped the kettle on my own foot when I turned round to yell at him.

Another person I got to know when I went walking was that funny little fellow who made his living by writing beautifully. He was what is called a 'scribe.' Did I tell you that I wondered at the words and the writing when I saw the Petition that went to Sydney about Will's Ticket? Well I asked the lawyer about it and he told me about Scribbler. That was the only name I ever found out for this friend.

Scribbler was a forger who came to the colony as a convict. He had worked for lawyers in London who needed documents prepared that had to look very old or be written by a certain person. He could write in any style needed. In a way he was an artist but because he was copying other people's stuff, not making new stuff, he found himself on a transport ship to Sydney Town.

I talked to him first on the day I visited *Garroorigang*, a fairly new house on the Braidwood road. I had heard about the beautiful garden and that is where I met Scibbler.

"Good morning," I said. "Isn't it a beautiful day to be visiting such a beautiful garden."

He looked so surprised I'd spoken that for a minute I thought he'd run away.

"Yes, ma'am, you're right. It is a beautiful garden."

"You sound like a Londoner."

"Oh yes, I am. You're not though. Irish I think."

"Yes … can't hide that." He took a few steps away from me so I touched his shoulder. "I'm Catharine Maber. I want to thank you for the Petition you wrote for me when my husband Will got his Ticket."

He stopped and stared at me. "Oh copying is my job, the Lawyer chooses the words."

"That may be so but I'm sure your elegant writing was as important as the words. I'm sure that's why I got Will out so quickly."

"No, no," he muttered but I could see he was pleased. I tried a bit more blarney.

"You know I didn't think anyone could write as clearly as you do. My writing looks like a spider that dipped its legs in the ink then walked across the page."

That made him laugh. "Oh, ma'am, I practised a lot to learn my job."

I was now feeling quite bold. "What's your name? I'd like to know how to address you."

"Ah I've only one name here, Mrs Maber. Just call me Scribbler. I'm glad I helped you. If you ever want a special letter written I will be glad to do it and there is no charge for a friend."

I didn't need to write letters to anyone but I thanked him and said that if I needed help I'd let him know. He tipped his hat to me and hurried away. I don't think he was used to talking to people.

From then on if I saw him in the street I always spoke to him. Gradually he became comfortable with me. We discovered that in London we had lived in the same area. He knew Dews Hosiery shop where I had worked. We might even have passed each other in the street. After that we were friends and always stopped for a chat when we met. If I was puzzled about a new word I'd read in the newspaper, I'd save it up till I saw him and he'd explain it. He was as interested in words as I was.

Life's funny. Here we were in the same little town on the bottom of the world, having both come from the biggest city of all that perches on the top of the world. Yes … Life is funny.

I have to admit that my Will got into strife from time to time. He would have a bit too much to drink or he'd try to help people, without questioning if what they were doing was sensible. Once he agreed to carry a large piece of bacon home to a mate's house without stopping to wonder how that fellow could have afforded it. Of course it was stolen and a policeman stopped Will and asked questions he couldn't answer. Luckily it was sorted out, but not before news of it got into the papers.

When things went wrong outside a pub at closing time, he was often blamed because he was strong and forgot that others weren't. I think a couple of Policemen remembered him kindly from his time on Cockatoo, so they'd pull him out of rows before he got too far in. Nothing really serious happened though, so all was well.

Beth left school at about the same time as I got the sewing machine. She learnt to use it and she tried to teach Ann, but for some reason Ann couldn't get the hang of her hands and feet working at different rates.

Beth came with me a few times when I worked as a maid for some of the gentry. Once she felt confident, she applied for a job as a maid at Mandelsohn's Hotel. She got it straight away thanks to references from Mr Senden, the teacher, and Mrs Walsh, the Lawyer's wife. I had taught Beth well and she was popular both with her boss and with visitors, many of whom tipped her well. There was a new sewing machine at the hotel, so her ability to use it meant that she had a job for as long as she wanted one.

She stayed there happily for a number of years but at last, of course, an elderly couple, who were frequent Hotel guests, took a fancy to her and persuaded her to come and work for them on their large and lonely property south of Goulburn. She was nearly twenty by then. We didn't want her to go but she had met their son once or twice and fancied her chances of marriage. By then, it was clear that Ann spent more time with Liam (who didn't live at home any more) than with Beth. Our daughter began to look for new friends and a new sort of life.

Just before she left, something happened that got everybody in Goulburn very excited. The Government in Sydney made a proclamation that Goulburn was now a City. It was the first inland City ever named in this new country. It was growing all the time and now had a Cathedral and a Bishop as well as lots of businesses. Will and I chose well when we decided to make Goulburn our home.

Beth's new employers came to town for the celebrations and we met them. They were very pleasant people. When they left our daughter went with them. A few months later we had a letter to say that she was married to their son. As soon as we heard that Beth was married we needed to write a letter. I talked to Scribbler and he took down what we wanted to say. I wrapped the paper inside a piece of fabric with all the coins from my special purse then posted it to the only address I had. We never had an answer. I can't be sure that she got it.

We never saw or heard from Beth again. The roads were bad and only went about half way to where she was living in the mountains. I lost my second daughter. I don't even know if she had any children. Long, long later we heard that she had died in childbirth and we felt that must be true, because Beth wouldn't have forgotten her family.

All my girls gone. First of all sister Lizzie, whose button I still treasured, then Louisa from the Manor and little Lucy in Dublin. My own two little Australians, sweet, fragile Jane and bonny Beth. I asked God once why I was so unlucky. I didn't get a direct answer but when I look back at my life I know that I have much to be thankful for. In particular I was blessed by my 'almost-daughter' Ann Surrey. She was a special girl and long before she married Liam she was a friend and companion to me. She still is.

I didn't know it at the time, but we were on the brink of two very difficult years. I missed Beth badly but at the same time I was glad that she didn't have to know about our troubles. Ann was caught up in the middle of them, so we just helped each other.

Sport was big in the town. Will played cricket with the men's team, Liam led the boys' team then moved into the men's team. At first both Beth and Ann sat with me on the sidelines to cheer our men, then it was only Ann. Round about this time a cricket team came out from England to play against the colonials in the Domain in Sydney. It was a one day match with a single innings for each team. My men simply had to go.

Liam was given time off work because his boss, a cricket fan, was going too. My boy couldn't afford coach fares so he walked when he couldn't get a free ride, but I had some savings in my special purse so Will travelled by coach. When they got back they talked about nothing else till Ann and I were driven crazy. Do you know, neither of them could ever tell me clearly which team had won the day! It didn't seem to matter.

Sport! What a lot of fuss over a game. If it wasn't cricket or football it was boxing.

Will encouraged Liam to join a 'secret' boxing group set up by a few 'big-wigs'. Some of these men even proclaimed at Council and Church meetings that boxing was an undesirable activity! None-the-less they did nothing to stop it. They never missed a bout. They all enjoyed watching young men fight each other.

Our lad was really good at it, though Ann and I hated watching his matches. Liam was tall and skinny with long arms that seemed to give him an advantage and he moved quickly. From the time he could walk he preferred to run and all that exercise seemed to give him a natural skill at sports. He only had one other interest – girls. He used to talk about several but it soon became obvious that Ann Surrey was his choice. We were both very pleased. I loved Ann and we had known her most of her life. We felt that she would make our son a good wife.

Everyone in Goulburn knew that young William Maber and Ann Surrey were a pair. Now twenty-four and long since having left home, Liam had a steady job so I couldn't understand why they didn't marry, especially, when their son arrived. What was going on?

Finding the answer to that question was a terrible shock. Late in 1867, Liam was arrested and thrown into jail to await trial for rape, a crime for which he could be hanged. I couldn't believe it. Ann had found out that he was playing around with some other girl so told him to get out of her life. A week or two later the girl accused him of rape and the police took action. Ann brought me the news.

Neither Will nor I could believe that our son would do such a dreadful thing. We hung our heads in shame. How could he do something the thought of which horrified us both? I started reliving the awful events of that long gone new year.

When we found out the name of the woman involved it got worse. Her name was Sarah Wildgust. She was only fifteen years old and had for a while lived with me! She'd been in jail three times. She'd lost touch with her parents and had nowhere to live, so I took her in and said that if she did a bit of work for me it would pay for her keep. Here was me trying to do her a good turn, while my son was treating her like rubbish. Compared with other girls, I could see that Sarah was fairly knowing for her age but Liam hadn't lived with us for years. I didn't even know they knew each other.

Will did his best to comfort me, but he was so shattered by the news of his son's disgrace that a couple of days later he made a swag out of a few clothes and a blanket and said he was going away for a while.

"I can't look anyone in the eye," he said. "My son a rapist … … I know that there's no bootmaker in Young at present so I'll go and work there over the summer and help the junior cricket team. I'll come back when things settle down."

I was very hurt that he left me in the middle of such a mess but Ann and the baby came to live with me, so perhaps it was good that we were alone. We dreaded the trial. How much more horrible could this story get?

Liam was fortunate. Something had happened between him and that girl but what and when and where I don't know. In court it came out that she had been familiar with men when she'd been in jail. There was so much evidence of bad behavior against her that in the end the court threw out her complaint. Liam was saved from complete disgrace, but that didn't alter the fact that while he fooled around with Sarah, he'd been playing fast and loose with the affections of Ann, one of the best girls in town.

As soon as I got my son alone I told him in no uncertain terms what I thought of him. I used language I'd learnt at the Factory — language he'd never heard from me before. I told him that if he was a real man he would go to Ann and ask for forgiveness. I wanted a daughter named Ann and I wanted their child to know that I was Gran.

Liam was shocked by my fury and my language. Later he told me he couldn't think how I could use such words. It shocked him so deeply that it made him very cautious about his behaviour in future. When I was around he became a bit careful about saying or doing anything that I mightn't like.

Liam eventually followed my advice, but it took him quite a time to win Ann back. It wasn't till August 1869 that she married him and their son was christened. They named him William Abraham, which I thought was daft, but in the end it didn't matter because he was always called Billy. A couple of months later their daughter Elizabeth Jane arrived.

I was really pleased that they chose both of those names and I was even more pleased that they always called the little one Jane. Thinking about it has reminded me it was the year of the big snowfall. Will and I got so excited that we rushed outside and played like kids. We hadn't seen snow since we left England. Liam and Ann were too busy with their new little daughter to join us. They just stood inside and laughed but little Billy toddled out to help us build a snowman.

Little Billy was my delight. Everyone spoilt him but I was the person he followed around. He was my shadow. As soon as he could walk he invented a game. He would pull my skirt then waddle away from me. Of course I always followed and scooped him up for a kiss and a cuddle. The game lasted for years. He found out that by running he could get further away from me and then the cuddle would be better. By the time he was four or five he was so good at running that I sometimes had trouble catching up. I called him my little runner and turned the game around.

"Billy," I'd call. "Run over to your Mam and ask her for a potato." Or I might say "Run to Pop and ask for the shoes he is mending for me."

No matter what I wanted he would run straight off and do it. Even now he is the best of the grandchildren at doing jobs for me and he still likes to follow me when I leave the house on an errand. He is still my shadow.

Ann seemed to love babies. She couldn't stop having them. After Jane came Catherine then Henry, followed by Mary Anne, Robert and Ada (though those two died very soon after birth). Samuel and Alice came next, in fact Alice arrived yesterday.

While listing all these grandchildren I have jumped over many other things that happened so I must go back a bit, to the time when Liam was in trouble and Will had gone walkabout to Young. I must face the few facts I have about that senseless part of our lives.

Young! I never visited that town but I knew a bit about Agnes Stevenson. None of it was good. I'd heard about her behaviour in Yass Court when she and another woman were accused of theft. My friend, Mrs Slater, liked to sit in the gallery at the court when there was a case involving women. She went to Stevenson's trial. Agnes was one of those females expert at putting on a "sad and lost and lonely face". The Court fell for it so she got off. Will would have been like soft pastry in her hands.

Will said that when Liam was in jail he went there for work and I remember when he got back he brought a few shillings for my special purse. He was away right through the summer. I never knew that he knew Agnes Stevenson, even though her trial at Yass Court was in the papers just before Liam was arrested. News I didn't want to hear came through Liam after he was in jail. He always picked up a lot of tattle and passed it on to me.

Some fellow from Young told Liam that when his dad visited Young he lived at widow Stevenson's rooming house. He said that the widow recently told everyone that she was about to marry her lodger from Goulburn. I just said it was tosh and nonsense and to forget about it. Liam did. He never thought much about anything.

This gossip worried me. Our kids didn't know that Will and I weren't married. We vowed years ago never to tell them. I didn't want them poking and prying into our early days in Sydney. I knew full well that if Will had married Agnes then it was quite legal but I was very hurt. Why would he do it? We were happy and had a growing family. One day I asked him straight out if there was any truth in the story. It was a very strange tale.

It was a day when we'd gone for a walk and were down at Mulwaree Ponds looking for platypus. Two appeared and entertained us ducking and chasing each other up and down the pond. We were very quiet until Will bent his head close to mine.

"They make me think of us," he whispered. "They're really good friends and they trust each other but they have fun together, just like us."

I was surprised by his words. Agnes was always on my mind.

"Don't you agree?" he asked.

As I watched, the platypus slapped their tails once on the water and disappeared into their burrow. I decided they were saying *'ask him now'*.

"Are we always friends, Will?"

"Of course. I know I go away sometimes, but I always tell you everything about my trips."

"Were we friends when you left me while Liam was in jail and you went to Young and got yourself tied up with that other person? … Did you tell me about it when you came home? … What's the truth behind the tattle that William Maber married Agnes Stevenson?"

Will looked horrified. He clearly didn't know that I knew about Agnes. "What have you heard and who told you?"

"Our son heard about that woman when he was in jail. Just think how I felt when he told me that you were about to marry another woman – a woman who had been before the courts and was really dishonest."

Will hid his face in his hands. He didn't want to look at me .

We sat like that for quite a few minutes. I was glad we were outside where no one could hear us. Whatever the story was, I didn't want to share it with anyone.

Will sat up and took my hands. "This reminds me of when we were in Sydney and you had to tell me all the nasty bits about your life. It's my turn now to tell you about this nasty thing. The answer to your question *did I marry her*, is both yes and no. It began long before I visited Young."

That startled me, but at least he was talking. "Go on," I said.

"I guess it started on Cockatoo … One night I told a fellow bootmaker all about you and how you were working to get me a Ticket-of-Leave. That started him complaining about his wife and saying that he never wanted to see her again. That was so different to how I felt about you that I asked him a few questions. He didn't really tell me much except that SHE (I never heard her real name) was a witch. She lived out beyond Bathurst and he didn't want to go back there when he'd done his time."

"Why don't you leave her?" I asked.

"Yep, I could, but we married properly and if I disappeared she'd have the police on me."

"Poor old you," I said. I felt so sorry for him that I forgot our promise never to talk about our arrangements. I blurted out "Pity you're not like Cate and me. We didn't marry."

That surprised him.

"How come?" he asked. By then I remembered our promise so I just said, "We had our reasons." That's all I said. On the day I left Cockatoo he cornered me and asked if what I had said was true, that I wasn't a married man. I just said it was and left it at that.

I made my first trip to Young quite a while after I got back from Cockatoo. I found a rooming house (not as good as yours, but good enough for a few days) with widow Stephenson. When Liam was in trouble and I went over there again she saw me in the street and said:

"George was hoping you'd come and visit. He's in the workroom next door." I didn't know what she was talking about, Cate. I went to the workroom and there was that miserable git I knew on Cockatoo. He leaped to his feet, patted me on the back like an old friend and took me out to tour Young.

He walked fast but he talked faster. "As far as Young is concerned you and me are brothers. I had to get clear of that witch of a wife. I borrowed your name and came up here and found Agnes. I'd met her before, I knew she was the woman for me. She's smart and clever and knows how to get the best deal out of life. She was up on a fraud charge but she got off. I'm gunna marry her as soon as I've earned enough to get us to the new colony in the north. If you work with me for a while I'll save money quicker and we'll clear off."

Will stopped and looked at me. I couldn't believe what I had heard.

"Oh Will, she's awful and not to be trusted. I heard all about the time she was before the Yass Court. She got off but only because she played the innocent before the Judge. How could you be caught by her?"

"But I wasn't caught by her. It was him who locked me in. He'd been to Young before and always said his name was Maber. He borrowed my full name but said that the family always called him George."

For a long time there was silence by the platypus pond. I had to say something but all I managed was

"Go away out of that, Will. It's the stupidest story I ever heard … Do you mean … are you telling me that he married her using your name?"

"Yes."

"But he stole *your* name. Why didn't you stop him?"

"I couldn't. I'd have had to involve the police. I couldn't do that. It would've put him back in jail. It's been a log around my neck ever since. I stayed there and worked with him to get rid of him. I worked for practically nothing and hoped that he'd soon have enough saved to get away. He did, because the day before I set out for home, he filled in the forms for them to get married. After I got back here I heard that there was no longer a bootmaker in Young. They must've gone to Moreton Bay so I was free. I hoped you'd never get to hear about it."

Did I believe this tale? I've never been able to decide. It is the sort of daft thing Will would think was okay if he was helping a mate, but who was that mate? I never found out. I asked Will many times but he wouldn't say. His story was that the fellow was hiding from his real wife and scared what might happen if she found him. Will told me that if I even mentioned his name to anyone, his secret would get out and his witch of a wife would have him slung into jail for bigamy.

I sometimes thought I should go to Young and hunt around for the truth. In the end I didn't. It was better to hold on to my ever growing family, not dig up something that might destroy it. I must trust Will's promise never to lie to me. The one thing I do know is that after that long trip when Liam was in trouble, Will never went to Young again.

Gradually Will's long walks out into the countryside ceased. Instead, I took him with me on my explorations of Goulburn. It was like our courting days in Sydney. Such a lot was happening. One place we visited regularly was the new Church of England Cathedral. They built it around the old St Saviour's. They kept the name and lots of the bricks but the new building was made of sandstone and was beautiful and enormous. It must be ten years since they started and it isn't finished yet. I don't think I'll ever get to explore the inside of it.

I think the building has taken so long because there was a great rumpus about both the old and the new St Saviour's. I read about it in the newspapers. Archdeacon Puddicombe was in the middle of it. I don't really know anything about it but the Archdeacon was a nice fellow. He was always polite when we met.

It was during those walks I noticed that my man had lost his straight back. There were times when he seemed to tip forward. I'd bang him between his shoulders telling him to 'stand up tall'. He would, but the stoop came back again. Then I saw that one of his feet was dragging on the ground. Liam noticed too and told me that his Da's shoes were wearing oddly. We didn't know why these changes were happening so I stopped talking about them, though I could see that slowly they got worse.

Salt of the Earth

This patch will be a small piece of strong linen the reddy-brown colour of Goulburn soil and on it a white silhouette of me in my sun-bonnet, the one that I designed myself!

Once Liam and Ann were married, much of my time was taken up helping Ann with the babies as well as keeping money flowing in from my lodgers. I made clothes for the little ones and I still accepted any sewing jobs offered, all thanks to the treadle machine which was working as well now as when I first received it from my good friend Sarah Wilshire.

Goulburn was growing and growing. After years of talk and planning, in May of the year Liam and Ann married, the railway arrived. The opening was a very exciting event with Lord and Lady Belmore, arriving from Sydney on the first train to make a speech and accept flowers from the Mayor's wife. They also planted an oak tree in our Market Square which was then renamed Belmore Park.

Will and I went to watch but I wasn't impressed. The Governor, Lord Belmore was an Earl and his wife a Countess. Surely he should have been a Count or maybe she should have been an Earless but they were plain old Lord and Lady Belmore. I asked Scribbler about this title business but he couldn't explain it so I just said: "Another old-fashioned English notion."

Even more daft was the fact that the REAL first train had arrived in Goulburn two months earlier, in March. It carried a cricket team. That was really exciting, a full day of fun. The local team took on the visitors from Sydney. I can't remember who won but it was probably Goulburn, they had a good team. Liam was in it.

The Railway Station was a brand new, very fine red brick building. Will and I had watched it grow. It was very wide and had a smart ticket office and a waiting room for passengers. The platform was so long that even on the longest train all passengers could step directly from the carriage to the platform. Once I knew the timetable I was able to go down and watch people come and go and I often did.

With the railway station completed, they started another smaller building near the road. At first we couldn't decide what it was going to be, then we found out it was to be a house for the Station Master. It is the most beautiful house I have ever seen. It is red brick with stone at the corners and a tall roof with attic windows. The front door has a small porch with elegant wooden lace around the edge, all painted white to match the stone at the corners. I watched every brick go into it. When it was nearly finished they built the chimneys. Ooh, they are lovely. Tall, with interesting hats at the top. I said to Will, "Why weren't you a Station Master? We could have lived in a house like that."

He looked at me so sadly. "No railways when I first got to this place. How could I?"

I had been joking of course but he was so serious now. He rarely laughed. I felt that I should be more careful about my silly whims.

Opposite my dream house was a new big hotel called the Railway Hotel. It had a balcony all along the top floor that gave shade and shelter to people on the footpath. Not many of the other buildings had that. I approved of that building too.

One exciting thing that happened to me was writing a letter to the Editor of the Goulburn Evening Post. I didn't like the newspaper report of the time I took Mr Cleary, a big shop keeper, before the court.

I went into his shop to buy some tape and while I was choosing what I wanted, Cleary came out of the office and started to search me. What a cheek! He dragged my shawl off and patted me all over saying: "Can't trust her. She's probably drunk."

I was furious. I dropped sixpence on the counter, picked up the tape and walked out of the shop and straight to the police station. How dare he manhandle me and accuse me of being in liquor while he stank of the stuff. I accused him of assault. When the magistrate heard the case Cleary was fined for 'exaggerating his rights as a shopkeeper'. Serve him right. I never shopped in his store again.

The story of my trial was told in the paper and it suggested that I was drunk. That annoyed me. The only drunkard in the shop was Cleary himself.

I wrote the letter and asked Scribbler for help. He wanted to change the wording a bit but I wanted it to be my work so he copied it out, I signed it and it was published. When I saw it in the paper I was a bit sorry I hadn't let him make some changes. It didn't really say clearly what I had been trying to explain.

Still, it was a lark to see my name as a contributor to the paper. I did it because I needed to make it clear that I was an honest and sober person, even if my dear Will sometimes wasn't.

It was well I did this, because a month later I was asked to give evidence for an Auburn Street neighbour. Because of my letter, I'm sure that the magistrate would have known that I was a reliable person. The other witness in the case was my lodger, Alan Ramsay.

The man in the dock was accused of house-breaking and stealing and was jailed for six months. It was all a bit odd. I'd seen him snooping around the house when I was standing at my front door talking to my lodger. The Court said there was doubt about the man's guilt on the stealing charge but he had keys for the house in his pocket – keys that the owner hadn't given him. That meant, I suppose, that he had plans to come back for a spot of house-breaking another day. "Off to jail," they said.

My thoughtless, devil-may-care son, Liam, faced trouble again in the Courts just before his little son Henry was born. He went off on a night out with his mates and of course had too much to drink and was accused of helping himself from the till at the pub. He swore to me that he didn't and I believed him. Ever since his earlier trouble with the law, he had been very cautious about telling me lies. His mates all gave witness on his behalf but they weren't much use because they were drunk that night too. He was saved by his defendant, Mr Gannon, and his boss, Mr Gllespie.

Gillespie was brilliant. He stood up before the Magistrate and said that he'd known Liam since he was a boy and that he'd employed him for about 15 years. He said my Liam was the best apprentice he'd ever had. He said he was 'steady' though sometimes he played jokes on people and that he was a married man who sometimes went on a spree. He said such good things about Liam that the Bench refused to convict him.

Something similar happened to Will too. One evening he decided to visit the Kelly family and asked me to go with him but for some reason that I've forgotten, I didn't. My mistake!

He came home very late and in a very silly state, carrying two pairs of disgusting boots. He left them just inside our front door. He said he'd found them on a rubbish heap. Knowing the Kelly house as I did, I thought it could well have been in the kitchen!

"We've got a bet," he said. "Kelly says these boots are useless, I said they would be good for someone."

"Bet ya' can't clean 'em," said Kelly.

"Bet I can. I'll do it tomorrow. Then I'll give 'em to the first poor man I see."

"Yah," said Kelly. "Not even the poorest black feller in Goulburn would want those bits of rubbish."

We never found out who would have won that bet because the next day the Police came to visit us. Will was not in any state to say anything sensible. The Kellys had accused him of theft and of course the boots were inside our house.

The case ended up in the Court. Mr Gannon was on the Bench that day. He refused to believe the Kelly evidence because they were drunk and when the jury considered the matter, they acquitted Will. I was a bit surprised but very relieved.

Next time I passed Mr Gannon in the street I gave him a proper little bob. I thought that was the least I could do!

The young Maber family grew and grew. I felt that it was very unfair on Ann that Liam insisted on living in that pokey three-room house in Clifford Street. Many times I nagged Liam to move a bit out of town to a bigger house with space around it. He wouldn't. Ann was so patient. She never complained, so I did what I could to help, by having some of the children over to sleep with me if I didn't have lodgers.

Boxing was now an accepted sport so Liam trained Billy. His running and boxing improved every year. Built just like his Da, tall and skinny, Billy was very light on his feet. One or two men who watched him believed that he could have a good career in the ring, and even said that because he was so thin and so fast he should call himself Shadow Maber. If he does, I think it'd be a good name. It's what we all called him when he was little – 'Gran's shadow.'

My Will began to change. He no longer enjoyed even short walks. He lost interest in cricket and didn't go to watch the boxing bouts.

He seemed to live in the distant past. Every now and again he'd tell me stories about living in Bath and about his aunts and uncles who lived in Bathford. He would get angry and tell me again and again the tale of his best friend Joe Parfitt, who dobbed him in to the police when Will borrowed a coat to wear for a visit to his rich aunt. He said Joe did it because he was jealous of Will being better at cricket. Will was always in the team but Joe often missed out.

Isn't that word 'dobbed' funny? Scribbler told me about it. There is a thing called a dobby that weavers use to work on small patterns. Now we use it when someone weaves into a story bits that change it. Joe wove 'stole' into a story instead of 'borrowed'.

Will had another awful Bath story about a nasty lady called Mrs Andrew. She wanted him to make her a beautiful pair of shoes but only if he didn't charge her. She knew Will's aunt and had heard the story about what happened at Bathford.

She said, "If you make shoes for me and other people like them, you'll soon get enough orders to pay for mine."

He couldn't possibly do this. It was just after he'd been in jail because of Joe's coat. He had no money at all. She was so unreasonable that in the end he stole a cheese from her husband's shop. That cheese was a one-way-ticket to New South Wales.

When he talked about this event there was so much anger that I sometimes feared what he might do. To calm him I'd run over to Ann and borrow one of the little ones to come and sit on Pop's knee. That always worked. He always thought the child on his knee was either Liam or Beth and he forgot the sad past and played beautifully with them. He didn't live to know about the arrival of Ada, Samuel and Alice.

All this time Mr Gillespie visited Will. They had known each other since we first arrived and once or twice Will had worked for him. Liam told Gillespie that his Da didn't get out much anymore, so he'd come around and they'd yarn about making shoes and dealing with customers and about cricket and the new football game that was becoming popular. I think it was called rugby. I never saw a match but the men seemed to find it interesting. Scribbler did too and he would visit and talk to Will about it. The only other regular visitor was Hector Dallas. He and Will were great mates but I never liked the man. He was a clumsy fellow and visited our home to try and help when Will was on Cockatoo. I was very grateful for his friendship now.

Will was clearly less able to do anything active so I spent a lot of time at home with him. I'd buy the newspapers and read out interesting bits to him. He liked any sporting news and any gossip about our neighbours – in fact he liked anything as long as it didn't include any of us.

I usually kept an eye on reports in the papers about the Goulburn Municipal Council. A day or two after meetings, someone would write a story about what had happened. One of Will's cricket friends, George Richards, was quite an important person on the Municipal Council. He was a fellow who liked a good laugh and I knew him just a little because I'd seen him at cricket games. When I wrote that Cleary letter to the paper, he congratulated me and said something like:

"Never let newspapers get away with making a mess of a story."

One day I was out for a walk and I noticed George pacing up and down the street near the Cathedral. He seemed to be talking to himself. I walked past with a "Good morning" nod and was surprised when he fell into step with me. We walked a full block before he said anything.

"Are you planning any more letters to the newspaper, Mrs Maber?"

"Oh no," I said. "I only wrote once when I was angry about something."

"You don't have to be angry to do it, you know."

"Well I would. Anyway what have I got to write about?"

We walked on a bit further till he started again. "Do you read the parts in the paper about the Municipal Council?"

"Well yes, I do. I read it out to Will and we try to work out what they are planning."

"Did you read the most recent one?"

"Yes. It was about work on roads."

"You know, don't you, that I work for the Council."

"Yes, but I don't know what you do."

"One thing I do is to attend Council meetings and write the record of what happens."

"Well you'd know all about it then."

"Yes … After the last meeting the newspaper report was all wrong. I'm very angry about it!"

"Well then, write a letter to the editor."

"Oh I'd love to," he said, "but if I did I'd lose my job. I've written the letter but I'll have to find someone else to sign it."

He stopped talking for a while then suddenly took hold of my elbow and said: "Mrs Maber, would you let me put your name on that letter?"

I was amazed. "But, Mr Richards, wouldn't that be illegal?"

"Oh no," he said. "Not illegal, just a bit unusual. It's a sort of a joke. What do you think?"

It all seemed a bit odd but what harm could it do?

"I'll have to talk to Will," I said. "He likes to know in advance if any of us is about to appear in the paper. Leave it a day or two then visit us and show us the letter you want me to sign."

Well he did visit us. I told Will all about it and he didn't mind. He got on well with George. I saw the letter but I didn't understand it at all. It was all about stuff that didn't make sense to me, though I could tell that George didn't like two of the men on the Council, although he clearly had great respect for Mr Gannon, the Mayor. Well, we respected Mr Gannon too.

I read the strange letter a couple of times then asked Mr Richards what gave me the right to complain about the Council.

"You're a citizen of this city, Mrs Maber. You pay your dues and you aren't afraid to speak up for yourself. It's people like you and Will that are the foundation of this new country. I know that you fought to give your children and grandchildren the best start in life that is possible. You are the salt of the earth."

That was a long and fairly grand speech and I needed to think about it, to work it all out, so I signed the letter and he left.

It got into the paper and several people asked me how I'd come to write such a long and unusual letter. I just looked at them and didn't answer.

I talked about it to Scribbler when he visited and his advice was not to do it again.

"If people want to make mischief," he said "they should be honest enough to sign their own letters."

I asked him what 'salt of the earth' meant. He wanted to know where I had heard it so I told him about the grand speech.

"He's right, you know. All we convicts have had a part to play in creating Australia and people like you, who worked non-stop to improve your lot, have given it a good start. Most everything that lives needs salt and we hard workers are the salt this Australian colony needed."

Phew, I had to think about that too. After Scribbler left I asked Will what he thought.

"He's right, Cate. You are the steady centre of my family. When we got together I promised to look after you but really, you have looked after me. I love you and I'm proud of you."

I've thought about all of this often and I came to understand what Scribbler and George said, but I liked Will's version best.

My dear Will was not doing well. As I feared, our time together ended swiftly. Suddenly he was so stiff that he couldn't leave his bed. He didn't have arthritis like me, it was something else. I couldn't nurse him myself and there was no room in Liam's house for a sick man. Will's friend Hector Dallas helped out. He came around one day with a couple of strong lads and they carried Will on his mattress to Hector's home in Cowper Street. It was not far from Liam's and I moved to a small house close by in Ellesmere Street.

Hector, Ann and I did the nursing and kind Dr Gentle visited. He said that the problem was old age, combined with the effect of all the sad and cruel things that had happened to Will before we were married. The youngsters were all very upset.

William's life ended on 4 March 1880. Rev Soares buried him in the Mortis Street cemetery in Goulburn. I want to mark his grave with a stone but we haven't been able to afford it yet.

So my best friend died. The one person I always trusted from the day I told him my ugly life story till the day he died. I know he wasn't perfect but who is?

When I took his name he promised never to lie to me: "If you ask me a question I'll give you a truthful reply. If you think you won't like the answer then don't ask the question." I never forgot those words and I don't believe he ever lied to me, though sometimes I think he only told me part of the story. Despite this, I was always sure that he hadn't committed that robbery back in 1852, which is why I worked non-stop to get him out of jail.

It was also why, deep-down, I came to believe that he hadn't married Agnes Stephenson in 1868, and in the end I had some evidence to prove it!

I decided that I needn't to go back to a four-roomed house, so I went to see Mr Gillespie about leasing a two-roomed place he owned in Bourke Street that was close to Liam and Ann. While we were chatting he began to speak of his Factory.

"I've recently taken on a new worker who came down from Queensland," he said. "He's a handy young bloke but needs more training. I suggested to him that he could find lodging with you, but it turns out he has friends here so he is okay. When I mentioned your name he said he'd done his apprenticeship with George Maber."

It was such a shock hearing that name that I only just stopped myself from falling over.

"Are your all right Mrs Maber? Is George Maber related to your husband?"

"I'm all right," I said. "I … it … it was a shock to hear of another Maber. As far as I know my Will was the only Maber in Australia."

"It's an unusual name," said Mr Gillespie, "so I thought I'd ask."

Nothing else was said but the more I think, the more I have come to believe that George Maber, the Moreton Bay bootmaker, was Will's nameless mate who married Agnes Stephenson.

It was hard to lose him. I missed him a lot and still do. There's no one to tell about new buildings. We'd been watching the new Post Office grow but he missed seeing that grand building finished. I had no one to share silly jokes with. No one to talk to about the kids. It was lonely. I just had to learn how to see out the rest of my life alone.

I decided that I needn't live in my big house so I moved to a two-roomed place in Bourke Street. It was owned by Mr Gillespie and he only charged me a little bit of rent. It was close to Liam and Ann so Jane, now eleven, came to live with me.

I began to recover my energy. I knew I could still deal with lodgers so I moved back to a four-room house in Auburn Street. Jane came with me and Billy did too, whenever he wasn't travelling to boxing events. I soon had a lodger and Jane did well with the sewing machine. I felt very confident that I would stay in that house forever.

In the end, taking in lodgers got me into trouble. The last one I ever had (a fellow called Reardon) didn't see why he should pay his rent. When I asked for the seven shillings and sixpence he owed me he grabbed and hurt me, so I reported him to the police. He ended up in jail with three months hard labour, but I was very shaken by the whole thing. I didn't even enjoy seeing the story of his jailing in the paper.

Liam and Ann wanted me to shift into their house. I knew it wouldn't work. Their house is too small. Ann is a great comfort to me but it's quite a long walk from her house to mine, especially as she comes every day, so I did move after all. I moved to number twenty-two Clifford Street. That's where I am now.

This is a big house with four rooms and a kitchen as well. My friend Mrs Slater lives here. She took me in as a lodger and all she asks for as payment is that Jane do her pile of mending and darning. What a good friend to have. Ann sends in my main meal every day. I am very happy. I can still get up but I do find the bed comfier. The little ones sit on the bed and I can tell them stories and teach them the oranges and lemon song. It's surprising but I can still sing a bit and they all think it's fun to join in.

The Silken Cord

The end of my story is close. I will not dream another patch. I need to create the beautiful cord that will show the reader of my quilt how to follow the story. First of all I will plait all the left over embroidery silks I have in my box and at its end I will attach Lizzie's button. Then I will use my crochet hook to wind gold and silver threads through the plait, making sure that as I attach plait to quilt it traces the order of my memories. The cord will start in the centre on the soft yellow and green patch and move out until it has been on every patch I have made. You must follow it yourself if you wish to know it's route.

I sit here remembering my life and I wait for one grandchild to show some interest in the beginning of the Maber story in Will's promised land or, as they would say, in Australia. They'd rather hear what it's like in Sydney. They don't believe that I started work before I was ten and spent years as a skivvy sleeping on the bottom shelf of a cupboard. Working like that for other people doesn't make sense to them. They're not curious about the things that happened that caused us to be sent to New South Wales. Such things are too close. They understand how we came here and they know that we both spent seven years working for free settlers until we got our freedom but they don't want to know the details either before or after we made the mistake that sent us here. Many of their friends have the same background and I think they have all decided that it doesn't matter and is best forgotten.

This reminds me of Harriet who was on the ship with me and who used to say, "That is the past and it doesn't matter anymore." Maybe she was right and maybe my grandchildren are too.

Will and I laid the foundation of a family on this side of the world. How we got here, how we met, what bad things happened before we met won't alter the story of our children and grandchildren. I hope they all have healthy and happy lives and look back with pleasure on Will and me, without being saddened by the rotten experiences we both had. Let them remember us as that funny old pair, Pop and Gran, who always had time for a game or a cuddle and always found a penny or a sweetie for an empty pocket.

It's funny to think that if I had told any of them this story as I dreamed of my quilt, they would know our secrets. Well, unless they understand a quilt they can't see, they'll never know, and it doesn't matter a bit!

My fingers are so stiff now that I can scarcely hold the young ones hands. I can no longer lift them up. My back and legs are stiff with arthritis. Sometimes I hate getting up in the morning because I'm dizzy. The thought of food doesn't interest me at all. Ann cooks lovely soup and Billy brings it to me, but I can't be bothered with it. I just have a cup of tea and close my eyes so that they'll think I'm asleep again.

Dr Gentle visits now and then but there is not much he can do for me, though the stuff he gives me to rub on my crooked joints helps a bit. It has a good clean smell. He calls it wintergreen. Mr Gillespie and Scribbler both drop in at least once a week and last week my horseback-rescuer friend sent his daughter over with a huge bunch of roses. I can smell them still.

Another year has started. It is 1884. There was a great bonfire down by the Mulwaree Ponds to celebrate. Billy told me that all the town went. I didn't care. My memories mean that I never celebrate new year. I don't think I'll see another but I don't mind.

Billy will be seventeen this year. He is growing up and I fear that he will leave Goulburn soon. He is often away with people who arrange boxing matches in other towns. He travels a lot and wins lots of fights but it is brutal – just his bare knuckles against the other person's. I hope he is successful and that he isn't injured badly in those fights. From what he tells me, he will soon be travelling outside New South Wales to other colonies.

Jane is fifteen. She still spends a lot of time with me and has taken over all the making and mending for the family. The sewing machine is hers now. I have taught her how to measure materials and how to arrive at a fair price for work she takes in. She can earn a living with that knowledge. She will be all right.

Catherine stays home and gives Ann the help she needs.

I can't persuade Liam to be strict about his children going to school regularly. It is just around the corner in Bourke Street and there are no fees. Liam simply can't be bothered. Henry started well and really enjoyed sums but now seems to run wild on the streets. Mary Anne misses school whenever she wants to. Sometimes she hides under my bed before I wake up and makes that an excuse for not going. The others are too young for school. Sam is a sturdy little boy who follows Henry everywhere and Alice isn't yet a year old.

My quilt is done. It's there for all to read if they know how. I've finished it which means that my story is finished.

I believe that I completed most of the things I set out to do during my life and I am sure that my decision to become Catharine Jane Maber was the right one for me.

It's time to rest.

--oOo--

Coda

1835 Catharine's arrest details:

On 26 January she pawned six pairs of stockings.

On 7 February the Dews dismissed her.

On 11 February she pawned the last two pairs of stockings.

On 20 February she was arrested and thrown into jail to await trial.

On 2 March she was tried at the Old Bailey.

On 16 April she sailed for NSW.

Catharine died at 22 Clifford St, Goulburn on 22 October 1884.

She was buried the next day at the Mortis Street Cemetery, the officiating clergyman being Archdeacon Puddicombe. No stone marks where either she or William lies.

Her last grandchild, Edith, was born on 29 September 1885.

Edith's mother, Ann, died when the child was three years old.

By about 1910 all of the grandchildren had left Goulburn. Two little boys, Catharine's great-grandchildren, were left, temporarily, in a Goulburn Boys Home. Temporary became permanent and luckily they were fostered by a successful businessman and butcher who lived in Kialla, a small village about 9 kms from Crookwell.

The little boys grew and prospered. They both married happily to Crookwell girls and each had a son and a daughter.

It was the son of one of those little boys who was my husband and who led me on the hunt for Catharine and William. My husband, William, was their great-great-grandson. The male line appears to have ended.

Bibliography

Manning Clark: "Telling the Story" 1976 being his final Boyer Lecture 1976. (An edited version of the lecture appeared in 2018 in THE AUSTRALIAN AUTHOR, Vol 50, No. 2)

Judith Flanders: The Victorian House (Published 2003)

Judith Flanders: The Victorian City (Published 2012)

Robert Hughes: The Fatal Shore (Published 1986)

Annette Salt: These Outcast Women – The Parramatta Female Factory 1821-1848 (Published 1984 by Hale & Ironmonger Pty. Ltd)

Ransome T Wyatt: The History of Goulburn N.S.W. (Published by the Municipality of Goulburn NSW in 1941)

Acknowledgments

My husband, William Maber, who did the original research to locate his great great grandparents and their descendants.

Patricia and Terrence Fearnley, who found the loose ends we couldn't locate and who made contact when they realised that Terry and William were cousins. Their detailed research in Goulburn and elsewhere was invaluable for the writing of this novel.

Paul Moncrieff, my artist brother, who made Catharine's dream about a quilt visible.

Glennys Marsden, *urger extraordinaire,* who found anonymous readers who gave frank and helpful comments when I had scarcely started.

Friends and family for encouragement and especially the patient readers – M Angus, S & P Vassis, P Moncrieff, C March, D Mildern, M. Stephens and J Murray. Some saw the roughest of rough first drafts and encouraged me to write more, then had the courage to read the next draft and the next and …

Helen Iles, who pointed me towards publication.

Char March, friend, poet, play-write who gave me no-nonsense professional advice and tempered criticism with enormous support.

The Local Studies Officer at the Goulburn Mulwaree Library and several of her volunteer, and particularly Fran O'Flynn who read a draft and offered pertinent comments.

Members of Historical Societies in Goulburn and unknown volunteers at places of Historical interest in Goulburn, all of whom readily shared their knowledge.

Peter Staples, who introduced me to Bathford and found the house where the first William may have been taken into custody by Constable Thatcher.

CHILDREN'S BOOKS WRITTEN BY FRANCES MABER

Willit's Friends (2006) – A baby wombat without his mother is led to safety by Willy Wagtail and other friends. *

Willit the Wombat Grows Up (2007) – Willit's aunt looks after him then when he is two years old he goes off alone to dig his own burrow.

Willit the Amazing Wombat (2008) – Willit finds a mate and discovers that family life is busy when a joey needs to be rescued.

Colour Willit's Walkabout (2018) – A colouring-in book including old and new friends.*

Bush Surprises (2015) – A Hidden Alphabet about bush plants and creatures. Twenty-six rhymes to have fun with.

Bush Christmas (2017) – A lonely old man preparing for Christmas visitors is helped by a Bush Angel and a small donkey.

(* These 2 books are available from Booktopia and from the distributor Woodslane – www.woodslane.com.au)

Purchase also possible from: www.willitthewombat.com or rrcompany@iinet.net.au

All the books are illustrated in colour and black-and-white by artists Alexander and Jennifer Hills.

Proceeds from all these books goes to the The Wombat Foundation for research and care of Northern Hairy Nosed Wombats. www.wombatfoundation.com.au

About the Author

Frances Maber was born in England but educated in Australia.

She was a high school teacher, a Senior Executive in the Commonwealth Public Service and a University Registrar. She was awarded the OBE for services to education in 1979.

She gave up full-time work in 1991 since when she has been a writer.

She began publishing for children in 2006, her theme being wombats and the bush. She was blessed in six publications by having found Alexander and Jennifer Hills to do the illustrations. Profits from the sale of all the books goes to the Wombat Foundation for research and care of the endangered Northern Hairy Nosed Wombats.

In between wombats, she was involved in the search for her husbands' forebears. The hunt began in 1975 but wasn't completed until 2009. The information gained was always skeletal but Frances believed that there was a story to be told and she felt that Catharine herself was the person to tell it.

Remembering Catharine is Frances' first novel.

www.ingramcontent.com/pod-product-compliance
Lightning Source LLC
Chambersburg PA
CBHW071451080526
44587CB00014B/2072